HCISSP
Complete Self-Assessm

The guidance in this Self-Assessment is based on HCISSP best practices and standards in business process architecture, design and quality management. The guidance is also based on the professional judgment of the individual collaborators listed in the Acknowledgments.

Notice of rights

You are licensed to use the Self-Assessment contents in your presentations and materials for internal use and customers without asking us - we are here to help.

All rights reserved for the book itself: this book may not be reproduced or transmitted in any form by any means, electronic, mechanical, photocopying, recording, or otherwise, without the prior written permission of the publisher.

The information in this book is distributed on an "As Is" basis without warranty. While every precaution has been taken in the preparation of he book, neither the author nor the publisher shall have any liability to any person or entity with respect to any loss or damage caused or alleged to be caused directly or indirectly by the instructions contained in this book or by the products described in it.

Trademarks

Many of the designations used by manufacturers and sellers to distinguish their products are claimed as trademarks. Where those designations appear in this book, and the publisher was aware of a trademark claim, the designations appear as requested by the owner of the trademark. All other product names and services identified throughout this book are used in editorial fashion only and for the benefit of such companies with no intention of infringement of the trademark. No such use, or the use of any trade name, is intended to convey endorsement or other affiliation with this book.

Copyright © by The Art of Service
http://theartofservice.com
service@theartofservice.com

Table of Contents

About The Art of Service	7
Acknowledgments	8
Included Resources - how to access	8
Your feedback is invaluable to us	10
Purpose of this Self-Assessment	10
How to use the Self-Assessment	11
HCISSP Scorecard Example	13
HCISSP Scorecard	14
BEGINNING OF THE SELF-ASSESSMENT:	15
CRITERION #1: RECOGNIZE	16
CRITERION #2: DEFINE:	23
CRITERION #3: MEASURE:	34
CRITERION #4: ANALYZE:	46
CRITERION #5: IMPROVE:	54
CRITERION #6: CONTROL:	66
CRITERION #7: SUSTAIN:	76
HCISSP and Managing HCISSP Projects, Criteria for HCISSP Project Managers:	102
HCISSP: Planning Process Group	103
HCISSP: Cost Management Plan	105
HCISSP: Quality Metrics	107

HCISSP: Team Member Status Report	109
HCISSP: Human Resource Management Plan	111
HCISSP: Work Breakdown Structure	113
HCISSP: HCISSP Project Portfolio management	115
HCISSP: Milestone List	117
HCISSP: Lessons Learned	119
HCISSP: Risk Register	121
HCISSP: Stakeholder Management Plan	123
HCISSP: Activity Duration Estimates	125
HCISSP: Team Performance Assessment	127
HCISSP: Risk Data Sheet	128
HCISSP: Network Diagram	130
HCISSP: Procurement Audit	132
HCISSP: Team Directory	133
HCISSP: Executing Process Group	135
HCISSP: Stakeholder Analysis Matrix	137
HCISSP: Communications Management Plan	139
HCISSP: Assumption and Constraint Log	141
HCISSP: Roles and Responsibilities	143

HCISSP: Formal Acceptance	145
HCISSP: Quality Audit	146
HCISSP: Requirements Management Plan	149
HCISSP: Risk Management Plan	151
HCISSP: Closing Process Group	153
HCISSP: Activity Cost Estimates	155
HCISSP: Requirements Documentation	157
HCISSP: Activity Resource Requirements	159
HCISSP: HCISSP Project Scope Statement	161
HCISSP: Contract Close-Out	163
HCISSP: Activity List	164
HCISSP: Schedule Management Plan	166
HCISSP: Probability and Impact Assessment	168
HCISSP: WBS Dictionary	170
HCISSP: Cost Estimating Worksheet	173
HCISSP: Probability and Impact Matrix	175
HCISSP: Process Improvement Plan	177
HCISSP: Quality Management Plan	179
HCISSP: Stakeholder Register	181

HCISSP: Team Operating Agreement — 182

HCISSP: Contractor Status Report — 184

HCISSP: Scope Management Plan — 185

HCISSP: Cost Baseline — 187

HCISSP: Earned Value Status — 189

HCISSP: Responsibility Assignment Matrix — 190

HCISSP: Change Request — 192

HCISSP: Change Log — 194

HCISSP: Source Selection Criteria — 196

HCISSP: HCISSP Project Management Plan — 198

HCISSP: HCISSP Project Schedule — 200

HCISSP: HCISSP Project Performance Report — 202

HCISSP: Resource Breakdown Structure — 203

HCISSP: HCISSP Project or Phase Close-Out — 205

HCISSP: Requirements Traceability Matrix — 206

HCISSP: Variance Analysis — 208

HCISSP: Risk Audit — 209

HCISSP: Initiating Process Group — 210

HCISSP: Procurement Management Plan — 212

HCISSP: Decision Log	214
HCISSP: Duration Estimating Worksheet	216
HCISSP: Activity Attributes	218
HCISSP: HCISSP Project Charter	220
HCISSP: Change Management Plan	222
HCISSP: Team Member Performance Assessment	224
HCISSP: Issue Log	225
HCISSP: Monitoring and Controlling Process Group	226
Index	227

About The Art of Service

The Art of Service, Business Process Architects since 2000, is dedicated to helping stakeholders achieve excellence.

Defining, designing, creating, and implementing a process to solve a stakeholders challenge or meet an objective is the most valuable role... In EVERY group, company, organization and department.

Unless you're talking a one-time, single-use project, there should be a process. Whether that process is managed and implemented by humans, AI, or a combination of the two, it needs to be designed by someone with a complex enough perspective to ask the right questions.

Someone capable of asking the right questions and step back and say, 'What are we really trying to accomplish here? And is there a different way to look at it?'

With The Art of Service's Standard Requirements Self-Assessments, we empower people who can do just that — whether their title is marketer, entrepreneur, manager, salesperson, consultant, Business Process Manager, executive assistant, IT Manager, CIO etc... —they are the people who rule the future. They are people who watch the process as it happens, and ask the right questions to make the process work better.

Contact us when you need any support with this Self-Assessment and any help with templates, blue-prints and examples of standard documents you might need:

http://theartofservice.com
service@theartofservice.com

Acknowledgments

This checklist was developed under the auspices of The Art of Service, chaired by Gerardus Blokdyk.

Representatives from several client companies participated in the preparation of this Self-Assessment.

Our deepest gratitude goes out to Matt Champagne, Ph.D. Surveys Expert, for his invaluable help and advise in structuring the Self Assessment.

In addition, we are thankful for the design and printing services provided.

Included Resources - how to access

Included with your purchase of the book is the HCISSP Self-Assessment Spreadsheet Dashboard which contains all questions and Self-Assessment areas and auto-generates insights, graphs, and project RACI planning - all with examples to get you started right away.

How? Simply send an email to
access@theartofservice.com
with this books' title in the subject to get the HCISSP Self Assessment Tool right away.

You will receive the following contents with New and Updated specific criteria:
- The latest quick edition of the book in PDF
- The latest complete edition of the book in PDF, which criteria correspond to the criteria in...
- The Self-Assessment Excel Dashboard, and...
- Example pre-filled Self-Assessment Excel Dashboard to get familiar with results generation
- ...plus an extra, special, resource that helps you with project managing.

INCLUDES LIFETIME SELF ASSESSMENT UPDATES

Every self assessment comes with Lifetime Updates and Lifetime Free Updated Books. Lifetime Updates is an industry-first feature which allows you to receive verified self assessment updates, ensuring you always have the most accurate information at your fingertips.

Get it now- you will be glad you did - do it now, before you forget.

Send an email to **access@theartofservice.com** with this books' title in the subject to get the HCISSP Self Assessment Tool right away.

Your feedback is invaluable to us

If you recently bought this book, we would love to hear from you! You can do this by writing a review on amazon (or the online store where you purchased this book) about your last purchase! As part of our continual service improvement process, we love to hear real client experiences and feedback.

How does it work?
To post a review on Amazon, just log in to your account and click on the Create Your Own Review button (under Customer Reviews) of the relevant product page. You can find examples of product reviews in Amazon. If you purchased from another online store, simply follow their procedures.

What happens when I submit my review?
Once you have submitted your review, send us an email at review@theartofservice.com with the link to your review so we can properly thank you for your feedback.

Purpose of this Self-Assessment

This Self-Assessment has been developed to improve understanding of the requirements and elements of HCISSP, based on best practices and standards in business process architecture, design and quality management.

It is designed to allow for a rapid Self-Assessment to determine how closely existing management practices and procedures correspond to the elements of the Self-Assessment.

The criteria of requirements and elements of HCISSP have been rephrased in the format of a Self-Assessment questionnaire, with a seven-criterion scoring system, as explained in this document.

In this format, even with limited background knowledge of HCISSP, a manager can quickly review existing operations to determine how they measure up to the standards. This in turn can serve as the starting point of a 'gap analysis' to identify management tools or system elements that might usefully be implemented in the organization to help improve overall performance.

How to use the Self-Assessment

On the following pages are a series of questions to identify to what extent your HCISSP initiative is complete in comparison to the requirements set in standards.

To facilitate answering the questions, there is a space in front of each question to enter a score on a scale of '1' to '5'.

> 1 Strongly Disagree
>
> 2 Disagree
>
> 3 Neutral
>
> 4 Agree
>
> 5 Strongly Agree

Read the question and rate it with the following in front of mind:

'In my belief, the answer to this question is clearly defined'.

There are two ways in which you can choose to interpret this statement;
1. how aware are you that the answer to the question is clearly defined
2. for more in-depth analysis you can choose to gather evidence and confirm the answer to the question. This

obviously will take more time, most Self-Assessment users opt for the first way to interpret the question and dig deeper later on based on the outcome of the overall Self-Assessment.

A score of '1' would mean that the answer is not clear at all, where a '5' would mean the answer is crystal clear and defined. Leave emtpy when the question is not applicable or you don't want to answer it, you can skip it without affecting your score. Write your score in the space provided.

After you have responded to all the appropriate statements in each section, compute your average score for that section, using the formula provided, and round to the nearest tenth. Then transfer to the corresponding spoke in the HCISSP Scorecard on the second next page of the Self-Assessment.

Your completed HCISSP Scorecard will give you a clear presentation of which HCISSP areas need attention.

HCISSP
Scorecard Example

Example of how the finalized Scorecard can look like:

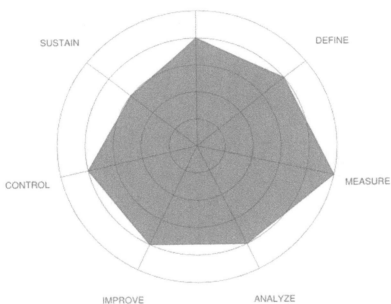

HCISSP Scorecard

Your Scores:

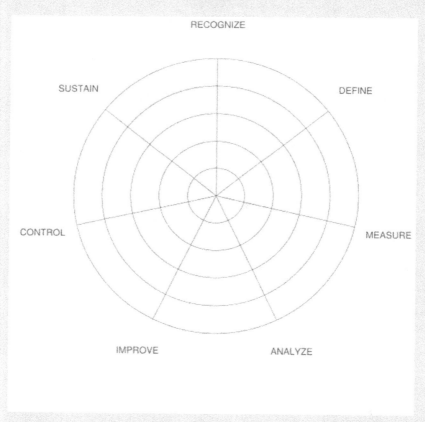

BEGINNING OF THE SELF-ASSESSMENT:

CRITERION #1: RECOGNIZE

INTENT: Be aware of the need for change. Recognize that there is an unfavorable variation, problem or symptom.

In my belief, the answer to this question is clearly defined:

5 Strongly Agree

4 Agree

3 Neutral

2 Disagree

1 Strongly Disagree

1. What are the business objectives to be achieved with HCISSP?
<--- Score

2. Are controls defined to recognize and contain problems?
<--- Score

3. How do you identify the kinds of information

that you will need?
<--- Score

4. Will it solve real problems?
<--- Score

5. What vendors make products that address the HCISSP needs?
<--- Score

6. What problems are you facing and how do you consider HCISSP will circumvent those obstacles?
<--- Score

7. Will HCISSP deliverables need to be tested and, if so, by whom?
<--- Score

8. Does HCISSP create potential expectations in other areas that need to be recognized and considered?
<--- Score

9. Are there HCISSP problems defined?
<--- Score

10. How can auditing be a preventative security measure?
<--- Score

11. How are the HCISSP's objectives aligned to the organization's overall business strategy?
<--- Score

12. How much are sponsors, customers, partners, stakeholders involved in HCISSP? In other words, what are the risks, if HCISSP does not deliver successfully?

<--- Score

13. What is the smallest subset of the problem we can usefully solve?
<--- Score

14. How do you assess your HCISSP workforce capability and capacity needs, including skills, competencies, and staffing levels?
<--- Score

15. What should be considered when identifying available resources, constraints, and deadlines?
<--- Score

16. How do we Identify specific HCISSP investment and emerging trends?
<--- Score

17. Can Management personnel recognize the monetary benefit of HCISSP?
<--- Score

18. How does it fit into our organizational needs and tasks?
<--- Score

19. Why do we need to keep records?
<--- Score

20. Does our organization need more HCISSP education?
<--- Score

21. How are we going to measure success?
<--- Score

22. Who had the original idea?
<--- Score

23. Think about the people you identified for your HCISSP project and the project responsibilities you would assign to them. what kind of training do you think they would need to perform these responsibilities effectively?
<--- Score

24. Consider your own HCISSP project. what types of organizational problems do you think might be causing or affecting your problem, based on the work done so far?
<--- Score

25. What would happen if HCISSP weren't done?
<--- Score

26. What information do users need?
<--- Score

27. What do we need to start doing?
<--- Score

28. What tools and technologies are needed for a custom HCISSP project?
<--- Score

29. Who defines the rules in relation to any given issue?
<--- Score

30. Have you identified your HCISSP key performance indicators?

<--- Score

31. What prevents me from making the changes I know will make me a more effective HCISSP leader?
<--- Score

32. What situation(s) led to this HCISSP Self Assessment?
<--- Score

33. Is it clear when you think of the day ahead of you what activities and tasks you need to complete?
<--- Score

34. How do you prevent errors and rework?
<--- Score

35. Do we know what we need to know about this topic?
<--- Score

36. Will new equipment/products be required to facilitate HCISSP delivery for example is new software needed?
<--- Score

37. Who needs to know about HCISSP ?
<--- Score

38. Are there any specific expectations or concerns about the HCISSP team, HCISSP itself?
<--- Score

39. What are the expected benefits of HCISSP to the

business?
<--- Score

40. What does HCISSP success mean to the stakeholders?
<--- Score

41. Are there recognized HCISSP problems?
<--- Score

42. For your HCISSP project, identify and describe the business environment. is there more than one layer to the business environment?
<--- Score

43. When a HCISSP manager recognizes a problem, what options are available?
<--- Score

44. What else needs to be measured?
<--- Score

45. As a sponsor, customer or management, how important is it to meet goals, objectives?
<--- Score

46. What training and capacity building actions are needed to implement proposed reforms?
<--- Score

47. How do you identify the information basis for later specification of performance or acceptance criteria?
<--- Score

48. Who else hopes to benefit from it?

<--- Score

49. Will a response program recognize when a crisis occurs and provide some level of response?
<--- Score

Add up total points for this section:
_____ = Total points for this section

Divided by: _____ (number of statements answered) = _____
Average score for this section

Transfer your score to the HCISSP Index at the beginning of the Self-Assessment.

CRITERION #2: DEFINE:

INTENT: Formulate the business problem. Define the problem, needs and objectives.

In my belief, the answer to this question is clearly defined:

5 Strongly Agree

4 Agree

3 Neutral

2 Disagree

1 Strongly Disagree

1. What is the minimum educational requirement for potential new hires?
<--- Score

2. How would you define the culture here?
<--- Score

3. Who defines (or who defined) the rules and roles?
<--- Score

4. What baselines are required to be defined and managed?
<--- Score

5. Have all of the relationships been defined properly?
<--- Score

6. Has the direction changed at all during the course of HCISSP? If so, when did it change and why?
<--- Score

7. Is there a HCISSP management charter, including business case, problem and goal statements, scope, milestones, roles and responsibilities, communication plan?
<--- Score

8. How is the team tracking and documenting its work?
<--- Score

9. How did the HCISSP manager receive input to the development of a HCISSP improvement plan and the estimated completion dates/times of each activity?
<--- Score

10. Is there a completed SIPOC representation, describing the Suppliers, Inputs, Process, Outputs, and Customers?
<--- Score

11. Has a high-level 'as is' process map been completed, verified and validated?
<--- Score

12. Has a team charter been developed and communicated?
<--- Score

13. Is the team adequately staffed with the desired cross-functionality? If not, what additional resources are available to the team?
<--- Score

14. What would be the goal or target for a HCISSP's improvement team?
<--- Score

15. How would one define HCISSP leadership?
<--- Score

16. Is a fully trained team formed, supported, and committed to work on the HCISSP improvements?
<--- Score

17. How will the HCISSP team and the organization measure complete success of HCISSP?
<--- Score

18. How do you keep key subject matter experts in the loop?
<--- Score

19. What are the compelling business reasons for embarking on HCISSP?
<--- Score

20. Who are the HCISSP improvement team members, including Management Leads and Coaches?
<--- Score

21. What specifically is the problem? Where does it occur? When does it occur? What is its extent?
<--- Score

22. How do senior leaders promote an environment that fosters and requires legal and ethical behavior?
<--- Score

23. When are meeting minutes sent out? Who is on the distribution list?
<--- Score

24. Is HCISSP Required?
<--- Score

25. Has the HCISSP work been fairly and/or equitably divided and delegated among team members who are qualified and capable to perform the work? Has everyone contributed?
<--- Score

26. Has a project plan, Gantt chart, or similar been developed/completed?
<--- Score

27. Are roles and responsibilities formally defined?
<--- Score

28. Is full participation by members in regularly held team meetings guaranteed?
<--- Score

29. Are business processes mapped?
<--- Score

30. Is the improvement team aware of the different versions of a process: what they think it is vs. what it actually is vs. what it should be vs. what it could be?
<--- Score

31. Is the scope of HCISSP defined?
<--- Score

32. Are accountability and ownership for HCISSP clearly defined?
<--- Score

33. What are the rough order estimates on cost savings/opportunities that HCISSP brings?
<--- Score

34. What defines Best in Class?
<--- Score

35. Has/have the customer(s) been identified?
<--- Score

36. Are there any constraints known that bear on the ability to perform HCISSP work? How is the team addressing them?
<--- Score

37. In what way can we redefine the criteria of choice in our category in our favor, as Method introduced style and design to cleaning and Virgin America returned glamor to flying?
<--- Score

38. Do we all define HCISSP in the same way?
<--- Score

39. Is HCISSP linked to key business goals and objectives?
<--- Score

40. Is the team sponsored by a champion or business leader?
<--- Score

41. Is the current 'as is' process being followed? If not, what are the discrepancies?
<--- Score

42. Are task requirements clearly defined?
<--- Score

43. Is there a completed, verified, and validated high-level 'as is' (not 'should be' or 'could be') business process map?
<--- Score

44. Are improvement team members fully trained on HCISSP?
<--- Score

45. What tools and roadmaps did you use for getting through the Define phase?
<--- Score

46. How often are the team meetings?
<--- Score

47. Does the team have regular meetings?
<--- Score

48. Is the HCISSP scope manageable?
<--- Score

49. Have the customer needs been translated into specific, measurable requirements? How?
<--- Score

50. Do the problem and goal statements meet the SMART criteria (specific, measurable, attainable, relevant, and time-bound)?
<--- Score

51. When is the estimated completion date?
<--- Score

52. Are approval levels defined for contracts and supplements to contracts?
<--- Score

53. Is HCISSP currently on schedule according to the plan?
<--- Score

54. Has the improvement team collected the 'voice of the customer' (obtained feedback – qualitative and quantitative)?
<--- Score

55. Are security/privacy roles and responsibilities formally defined?
<--- Score

56. Are Required Metrics Defined?
<--- Score

57. Is it clearly defined in and to your organization what you do?
<--- Score

58. How was the 'as is' process map developed, reviewed, verified and validated?
<--- Score

59. Will team members regularly document their HCISSP work?
<--- Score

60. Has everyone on the team, including the team leaders, been properly trained?
<--- Score

61. How will variation in the actual durations of each activity be dealt with to ensure that the expected HCISSP results are met?
<--- Score

62. What constraints exist that might impact the team?
<--- Score

63. Is there a critical path to deliver HCISSP results?
<--- Score

64. Have specific policy objectives been defined?
<--- Score

65. Have all basic functions of HCISSP been defined?
<--- Score

66. Are audit criteria, scope, frequency and methods defined?
<--- Score

67. Will team members perform HCISSP work when

assigned and in a timely fashion?
<--- Score

68. Are team charters developed?
<--- Score

69. How does the HCISSP manager ensure against scope creep?
<--- Score

70. Is the team formed and are team leaders (Coaches and Management Leads) assigned?
<--- Score

71. Has anyone else (internal or external to the organization) attempted to solve this problem or a similar one before? If so, what knowledge can be leveraged from these previous efforts?
<--- Score

72. What are the dynamics of the communication plan?
<--- Score

73. What key business process output measure(s) does HCISSP leverage and how?
<--- Score

74. If substitutes have been appointed, have they been briefed on the HCISSP goals and received regular communications as to the progress to date?
<--- Score

75. Are different versions of process maps needed to account for the different types of inputs?
<--- Score

76. What critical content must be communicated – who, what, when, where, and how?
<--- Score

77. In what way can we redefine the criteria of choice clients have in our category in our favor?
<--- Score

78. Are customers identified and high impact areas defined?
<--- Score

79. Is there regularly 100% attendance at the team meetings? If not, have appointed substitutes attended to preserve cross-functionality and full representation?
<--- Score

80. What are the boundaries of the scope? What is in bounds and what is not? What is the start point? What is the stop point?
<--- Score

81. What customer feedback methods were used to solicit their input?
<--- Score

82. Is data collected and displayed to better understand customer(s) critical needs and requirements.
<--- Score

83. What are the Roles and Responsibilities for each team member and its leadership? Where is this documented?

<--- Score

84. When was the HCISSP start date?
<--- Score

85. How and when will the baselines be defined?
<--- Score

86. Are there different segments of customers?
<--- Score

87. What organizational structure is required?
<--- Score

88. How can the value of HCISSP be defined?
<--- Score

89. Is the team equipped with available and reliable resources?
<--- Score

90. Are customer(s) identified and segmented according to their different needs and requirements?
<--- Score

Add up total points for this section:
_____ = Total points for this section

Divided by: _____ (number of statements answered) = _____
Average score for this section

Transfer your score to the HCISSP Index at the beginning of the Self-Assessment.

CRITERION #3: MEASURE:

INTENT: Gather the correct data. Measure the current performance and evolution of the situation.

In my belief, the answer to this question is clearly defined:

5 Strongly Agree

4 Agree

3 Neutral

2 Disagree

1 Strongly Disagree

1. How is progress measured?
<--- Score

2. Does HCISSP analysis isolate the fundamental causes of problems?
<--- Score

3. Is key measure data collection planned and executed, process variation displayed and

communicated and performance baselined?
<--- Score

4. Who participated in the data collection for measurements?
<--- Score

5. What is measured?
<--- Score

6. How is Knowledge Management Measured?
<--- Score

7. How are you going to measure success?
<--- Score

8. How large is the gap between current performance and the customer-specified (goal) performance?
<--- Score

9. Are there measurements based on task performance?
<--- Score

10. Among the HCISSP product and service cost to be estimated, which is considered hardest to estimate?
<--- Score

11. Why do measure/indicators matter?
<--- Score

12. What measurements are being captured?
<--- Score

13. Why Measure?

<--- Score

14. Is it possible to estimate the impact of unanticipated complexity such as wrong or failed assumptions, feedback, etc. on proposed reforms?
<--- Score

15. Is this an issue for analysis or intuition?
<--- Score

16. Are the units of measure consistent?
<--- Score

17. How are measurements made?
<--- Score

18. Is data collection planned and executed?
<--- Score

19. Which Stakeholder Characteristics Are Analyzed?
<--- Score

20. Does HCISSP systematically track and analyze outcomes for accountability and quality improvement?
<--- Score

21. How to measure lifecycle phases?
<--- Score

22. Are we taking our company in the direction of better and revenue or cheaper and cost?
<--- Score

23. Is Process Variation Displayed/Communicated?
<--- Score

24. Will We Aggregate Measures across Priorities?
<--- Score

25. How frequently do we track measures?
<--- Score

26. Was a data collection plan established?
<--- Score

27. What is the right balance of time and resources between investigation, analysis, and discussion and dissemination?
<--- Score

28. What are our key indicators that you will measure, analyze and track?
<--- Score

29. What are the costs of reform?
<--- Score

30. Meeting the challenge: are missed HCISSP opportunities costing us money?
<--- Score

31. What are the uncertainties surrounding estimates of impact?
<--- Score

32. Why identify and analyze stakeholders and their interests?
<--- Score

33. Which customers can't participate in our market because they lack skills, wealth, or convenient access

to existing solutions?
<--- Score

34. What potential environmental factors impact the HCISSP effort?
<--- Score

35. What charts has the team used to display the components of variation in the process?
<--- Score

36. What should be measured?
<--- Score

37. How do you identify and analyze stakeholders and their interests?
<--- Score

38. How will measures be used to manage and adapt?
<--- Score

39. Have the types of risks that may impact HCISSP been identified and analyzed?
<--- Score

40. What will be measured?
<--- Score

41. Why should we expend time and effort to implement measurement?
<--- Score

42. How do we do risk analysis of rare, cascading, catastrophic events?
<--- Score

43. Does the HCISSP task fit the client's priorities?
<--- Score

44. How to measure variability?
<--- Score

45. How Will We Measure Success?
<--- Score

46. How will effects be measured?
<--- Score

47. How do senior leaders create a focus on action to accomplish the organization s objectives and improve performance?
<--- Score

48. What are the types and number of measures to use?
<--- Score

49. Are key measures identified and agreed upon?
<--- Score

50. Who should receive measurement reports ?
<--- Score

51. Is performance measured?
<--- Score

52. What Relevant Entities could be measured?
<--- Score

53. Are process variation components displayed/ communicated using suitable charts, graphs, plots?
<--- Score

54. Can we do HCISSP without complex (expensive) analysis?
<--- Score

55. Does HCISSP analysis show the relationships among important HCISSP factors?
<--- Score

56. What particular quality tools did the team find helpful in establishing measurements?
<--- Score

57. What is an unallowable cost?
<--- Score

58. Is data collected on key measures that were identified?
<--- Score

59. How is the value delivered by HCISSP being measured?
<--- Score

60. How do you measure success?
<--- Score

61. Do we effectively measure and reward individual and team performance?
<--- Score

62. What are my customers expectations and measures?
<--- Score

63. What methods are feasible and acceptable to

estimate the impact of reforms?
<--- Score

64. What evidence is there and what is measured?
<--- Score

65. Are there any easy-to-implement alternatives to HCISSP? Sometimes other solutions are available that do not require the cost implications of a full-blown project?
<--- Score

66. Have you found any 'ground fruit' or 'low-hanging fruit' for immediate remedies to the gap in performance?
<--- Score

67. Are losses documented, analyzed, and remedial processes developed to prevent future losses?
<--- Score

68. How can we measure the performance?
<--- Score

69. How will success or failure be measured?
<--- Score

70. Have all non-recommended alternatives been analyzed in sufficient detail?
<--- Score

71. What to measure and why?
<--- Score

72. What about HCISSP Analysis of results?
<--- Score

73. How will your organization measure success?
<--- Score

74. How will you measure your HCISSP effectiveness?
<--- Score

75. Do we aggressively reward and promote the people who have the biggest impact on creating excellent HCISSP services/products?
<--- Score

76. Are high impact defects defined and identified in the business process?
<--- Score

77. Is a solid data collection plan established that includes measurement systems analysis?
<--- Score

78. What measurements are possible, practicable and meaningful?
<--- Score

79. What are the key input variables? What are the key process variables? What are the key output variables?
<--- Score

80. Is long term and short term variability accounted for?
<--- Score

81. When is Knowledge Management Measured?
<--- Score

82. What is the total cost related to deploying

HCISSP, including any consulting or professional services?
<--- Score

83. Are priorities and opportunities deployed to your suppliers, partners, and collaborators to ensure organizational alignment?
<--- Score

84. How frequently do you track HCISSP measures?
<--- Score

85. What are your key HCISSP organizational performance measures, including key short and longer-term financial measures?
<--- Score

86. Is there a Performance Baseline?
<--- Score

87. What data was collected (past, present, future/ongoing)?
<--- Score

88. Can We Measure the Return on Analysis?
<--- Score

89. How can you measure HCISSP in a systematic way?
<--- Score

90. What key measures identified indicate the performance of the business process?
<--- Score

91. What are measures?
<--- Score

92. How do we focus on what is right -not who is right?
<--- Score

93. Where is it measured?
<--- Score

94. Are the measurements objective?
<--- Score

95. Have the concerns of stakeholders to help identify and define potential barriers been obtained and analyzed?
<--- Score

96. What are the agreed upon definitions of the high impact areas, defect(s), unit(s), and opportunities that will figure into the process capability metrics?
<--- Score

97. Does the practice systematically track and analyze outcomes related for accountability and quality improvement?
<--- Score

98. Is the solution cost-effective?
<--- Score

99. Are you taking your company in the direction of better and revenue or cheaper and cost?
<--- Score

100. Which methods and measures do you use to determine workforce engagement and workforce satisfaction?

<--- Score

101. Have changes been properly/adequately analyzed for effect?
<--- Score

102. Which customers cant participate in our HCISSP domain because they lack skills, wealth, or convenient access to existing solutions?
<--- Score

103. Customer Measures: How Do Customers See Us?
<--- Score

104. Why do the measurements/indicators matter?
<--- Score

105. Do staff have the necessary skills to collect, analyze, and report data?
<--- Score

106. What has the team done to assure the stability and accuracy of the measurement process?
<--- Score

Add up total points for this section:
_____ = Total points for this section

Divided by: _____ (number of statements answered) = _____
Average score for this section

Transfer your score to the HCISSP Index at the beginning of the Self-Assessment.

CRITERION #4: ANALYZE:

INTENT: Analyze causes, assumptions and hypotheses.

In my belief, the answer to this question is clearly defined:

5 Strongly Agree

4 Agree

3 Neutral

2 Disagree

1 Strongly Disagree

1. How was the detailed process map generated, verified, and validated?
<--- Score

2. What did the team gain from developing a sub-process map?
<--- Score

3. Were any designed experiments used to generate additional insight into the data analysis?

<--- Score

4. What other jobs or tasks affect the performance of the steps in the HCISSP process?
<--- Score

5. Think about the functions involved in your HCISSP project. what processes flow from these functions?
<--- Score

6. What quality tools were used to get through the analyze phase?
<--- Score

7. Record-keeping requirements flow from the records needed as inputs, outputs, controls and for transformation of a HCISSP process. ask yourself: are the records needed as inputs to the HCISSP process available?
<--- Score

8. Is the HCISSP process severely broken such that a re-design is necessary?
<--- Score

9. Did any additional data need to be collected?
<--- Score

10. Where is the data coming from to measure compliance?
<--- Score

11. What conclusions were drawn from the team's data collection and analysis? How did the team reach these conclusions?

<--- Score

12. An organizationally feasible system request is one that considers the mission, goals and objectives of the organization. key questions are: is the solution request practical and will it solve a problem or take advantage of an opportunity to achieve company goals?
<--- Score

13. Was a cause-and-effect diagram used to explore the different types of causes (or sources of variation)?
<--- Score

14. What controls do we have in place to protect data?
<--- Score

15. Identify an operational issue in your organization. for example, could a particular task be done more quickly or more efficiently?
<--- Score

16. Were Pareto charts (or similar) used to portray the 'heavy hitters' (or key sources of variation)?
<--- Score

17. What process should we select for improvement?
<--- Score

18. Is the performance gap determined?
<--- Score

19. Is the suppliers process defined and controlled?
<--- Score

20. What are the best opportunities for value improvement?
<--- Score

21. How does the organization define, manage, and improve its HCISSP processes?
<--- Score

22. How is the way you as the leader think and process information affecting your organizational culture?
<--- Score

23. Did any value-added analysis or 'lean thinking' take place to identify some of the gaps shown on the 'as is' process map?
<--- Score

24. How do you measure the Operational performance of your key work systems and processes, including productivity, cycle time, and other appropriate measures of process effectiveness, efficiency, and innovation?
<--- Score

25. Were there any improvement opportunities identified from the process analysis?
<--- Score

26. Do our leaders quickly bounce back from setbacks?
<--- Score

27. Are gaps between current performance and the goal performance identified?
<--- Score

28. What were the financial benefits resulting from any 'ground fruit or low-hanging fruit' (quick fixes)?
<--- Score

29. What is the cost of poor quality as supported by the team's analysis?
<--- Score

30. Is the gap/opportunity displayed and communicated in financial terms?
<--- Score

31. Have the problem and goal statements been updated to reflect the additional knowledge gained from the analyze phase?
<--- Score

32. What are your current levels and trends in key HCISSP measures or indicators of product and process performance that are important to and directly serve your customers?
<--- Score

33. How do mission and objectives affect the HCISSP processes of our organization?
<--- Score

34. What tools were used to generate the list of possible causes?
<--- Score

35. How do we promote understanding that opportunity for improvement is not criticism of the status quo, or the people who created the status quo?
<--- Score

36. What were the crucial 'moments of truth' on the process map?
<--- Score

37. How often will data be collected for measures?
<--- Score

38. Have any additional benefits been identified that will result from closing all or most of the gaps?
<--- Score

39. What other organizational variables, such as reward systems or communication systems, affect the performance of this HCISSP process?
<--- Score

40. A compounding model resolution with available relevant data can often provide insight towards a solution methodology; which HCISSP models, tools and techniques are necessary?
<--- Score

41. Was a detailed process map created to amplify critical steps of the 'as is' business process?
<--- Score

42. What are the revised rough estimates of the financial savings/opportunity for HCISSP improvements?
<--- Score

43. When conducting a business process reengineering study, what should we look for when trying to identify business processes to change?

<--- Score

44. How do you use HCISSP data and information to support organizational decision making and innovation?
<--- Score

45. Do you, as a leader, bounce back quickly from setbacks?
<--- Score

46. What are the disruptive HCISSP technologies that enable our organization to radically change our business processes?
<--- Score

47. Can we add value to the current HCISSP decision-making process (largely qualitative) by incorporating uncertainty modeling (more quantitative)?
<--- Score

48. Do your employees have the opportunity to do what they do best everyday?
<--- Score

49. What does the data say about the performance of the business process?
<--- Score

50. What are our HCISSP Processes?
<--- Score

51. Think about some of the processes you undertake within your organization. which do you own?

<--- Score

52. Is Data and process analysis, root cause analysis and quantifying the gap/opportunity in place?
<--- Score

53. What successful thing are we doing today that may be blinding us to new growth opportunities?
<--- Score

54. What are your current levels and trends in key measures or indicators of HCISSP product and process performance that are important to and directly serve your customers? how do these results compare with the performance of your competitors and other organizations with similar offerings?
<--- Score

55. What tools were used to narrow the list of possible causes?
<--- Score

Add up total points for this section:
_____ = Total points for this section

Divided by: _____ (number of statements answered) = _____
Average score for this section

Transfer your score to the HCISSP Index at the beginning of the Self-Assessment.

CRITERION #5: IMPROVE:

INTENT: Develop a practical solution. Innovate, establish and test the solution and to measure the results.

In my belief, the answer to this question is clearly defined:

5 Strongly Agree

4 Agree

3 Neutral

2 Disagree

1 Strongly Disagree

1. Risk factors: what are the characteristics of HCISSP that make it risky?
<--- Score

2. How do we measure improved HCISSP service perception, and satisfaction?
<--- Score

3. Who will be using the results of the measurement

activities?
<--- Score

4. How significant is the improvement in the eyes of the end user?
<--- Score

5. How will the organization know that the solution worked?
<--- Score

6. At what point will vulnerability assessments be performed once HCISSP is put into production (e.g., ongoing Risk Management after implementation)?
<--- Score

7. Who are the people involved in developing and implementing HCISSP?
<--- Score

8. Is the implementation plan designed?
<--- Score

9. How can we improve performance?
<--- Score

10. What should a proof of concept or pilot accomplish?
<--- Score

11. How to Improve?
<--- Score

12. How do we keep improving HCISSP?
<--- Score

13. Are there any constraints (technical, political, cultural, or otherwise) that would inhibit certain solutions?
<--- Score

14. What are the implications of this decision 10 minutes, 10 months, and 10 years from now?
<--- Score

15. Who controls the risk?
<--- Score

16. What is the risk?
<--- Score

17. What tools were used to tap into the creativity and encourage 'outside the box' thinking?
<--- Score

18. How will you know when its improved?
<--- Score

19. What actually has to improve and by how much?
<--- Score

20. Are possible solutions generated and tested?
<--- Score

21. For decision problems, how do you develop a decision statement?
<--- Score

22. What communications are necessary to support the implementation of the solution?

<--- Score

23. Are we Assessing HCISSP and Risk?
<--- Score

24. Are the best solutions selected?
<--- Score

25. How can we improve HCISSP?
<--- Score

26. Risk events: what are the things that could go wrong?
<--- Score

27. How does the solution remove the key sources of issues discovered in the analyze phase?
<--- Score

28. Is there a high likelihood that any recommendations will achieve their intended results?
<--- Score

29. Do we get business results?
<--- Score

30. Is the solution technically practical?
<--- Score

31. How did the team generate the list of possible solutions?
<--- Score

32. What is the magnitude of the improvements?
<--- Score

33. In the past few months, what is the smallest change we have made that has had the biggest positive result? What was it about that small change that produced the large return?
<--- Score

34. How can skill-level changes improve HCISSP?
<--- Score

35. What to do with the results or outcomes of measurements?
<--- Score

36. What is HCISSP's impact on utilizing the best solution(s)?
<--- Score

37. How do you measure progress and evaluate training effectiveness?
<--- Score

38. How do you improve your likelihood of success ?
<--- Score

39. What improvements have been achieved?
<--- Score

40. Is the measure understandable to a variety of people?
<--- Score

41. What resources are required for the improvement effort?
<--- Score

42. Were any criteria developed to assist the team in testing and evaluating potential solutions?
<--- Score

43. How will you know that you have improved?
<--- Score

44. Can the solution be designed and implemented within an acceptable time period?
<--- Score

45. How do the HCISSP results compare with the performance of your competitors and other organizations with similar offerings?
<--- Score

46. Is a contingency plan established?
<--- Score

47. Why improve in the first place?
<--- Score

48. How important is the completion of a recognized college or graduate-level degree program in the hiring decision?
<--- Score

49. For estimation problems, how do you develop an estimation statement?
<--- Score

50. How will you measure the results?
<--- Score

51. Who will be responsible for making the decisions to include or exclude requested changes once HCISSP

is underway?
<--- Score

52. How do we go about Comparing HCISSP approaches/solutions?
<--- Score

53. How do we Improve HCISSP service perception, and satisfaction?
<--- Score

54. Who will be responsible for documenting the HCISSP requirements in detail?
<--- Score

55. Are improved process ('should be') maps modified based on pilot data and analysis?
<--- Score

56. How will the team or the process owner(s) monitor the implementation plan to see that it is working as intended?
<--- Score

57. What is the implementation plan?
<--- Score

58. What evaluation strategy is needed and what needs to be done to assure its implementation and use?
<--- Score

59. What needs improvement?
<--- Score

60. What do we want to improve?

<--- Score

61. What does the 'should be' process map/design look like?
<--- Score

62. Is the optimal solution selected based on testing and analysis?
<--- Score

63. What attendant changes will need to be made to ensure that the solution is successful?
<--- Score

64. How do we decide how much to remunerate an employee?
<--- Score

65. How does the team improve its work?
<--- Score

66. Are new and improved process ('should be') maps developed?
<--- Score

67. To what extent does management recognize HCISSP as a tool to increase the results?
<--- Score

68. Was a pilot designed for the proposed solution(s)?
<--- Score

69. Is there a small-scale pilot for proposed improvement(s)? What conclusions were drawn from the outcomes of a pilot?
<--- Score

70. What error proofing will be done to address some of the discrepancies observed in the 'as is' process?
<--- Score

71. Is pilot data collected and analyzed?
<--- Score

72. What can we do to improve?
<--- Score

73. What lessons, if any, from a pilot were incorporated into the design of the full-scale solution?
<--- Score

74. If you could go back in time five years, what decision would you make differently? What is your best guess as to what decision you're making today you might regret five years from now?
<--- Score

75. How will we know that a change is improvement?
<--- Score

76. What tools were used to evaluate the potential solutions?
<--- Score

77. How do you use other indicators, such as workforce retention, absenteeism, grievances, safety, and productivity, to assess and improve workforce engagement?
<--- Score

78. Is there a cost/benefit analysis of optimal solution(s)?

<--- Score

79. Describe the design of the pilot and what tests were conducted, if any?
<--- Score

80. What tools were most useful during the improve phase?
<--- Score

81. How Do We Link Measurement and Risk?
<--- Score

82. What is the team's contingency plan for potential problems occurring in implementation?
<--- Score

83. Is Supporting HCISSP documentation required?
<--- Score

84. How do we measure risk?
<--- Score

85. What were the underlying assumptions on the cost-benefit analysis?
<--- Score

86. How do you improve workforce health, safety, and security? What are your performance measures and improvement goals for each of these workforce needs and what are any significant differences in these factors and performance measures or targets for different workplace environments?
<--- Score

87. Is a solution implementation plan established, including schedule/work breakdown structure, resources, risk management plan, cost/budget, and control plan?
<--- Score

88. Who controls key decisions that will be made?
<--- Score

89. Does the goal represent a desired result that can be measured?
<--- Score

90. What went well, what should change, what can improve?
<--- Score

91. Do we cover the five essential competencies- Communication, Collaboration,Innovation, Adaptability, and Leadership that improve an organization's ability to leverage the new HCISSP in a volatile global economy?
<--- Score

92. How do we improve productivity?
<--- Score

Add up total points for this section:
_____ = Total points for this section

Divided by: _____ (number of statements answered) = _____
Average score for this section

Transfer your score to the HCISSP

Index at the beginning of the Self-Assessment.

CRITERION #6: CONTROL:

INTENT: Implement the practical solution. Maintain the performance and correct possible complications.

In my belief, the answer to this question is clearly defined:

5 Strongly Agree

4 Agree

3 Neutral

2 Disagree

1 Strongly Disagree

1. Against what alternative is success being measured?
<--- Score

2. What do we stand for--and what are we against?
<--- Score

3. Does the HCISSP performance meet the customer's requirements?

<--- Score

4. Who has control over resources?
<--- Score

5. How will the process owner and team be able to hold the gains?
<--- Score

6. How can we best use all of our knowledge repositories to enhance learning and sharing?
<--- Score

7. Why is change control necessary?
<--- Score

8. Is there a documented and implemented monitoring plan?
<--- Score

9. Where do ideas that reach policy makers and planners as proposals for HCISSP strengthening and reform actually originate?
<--- Score

10. Does the response plan contain a definite closed loop continual improvement scheme (e.g., plan-do-check-act)?
<--- Score

11. What should the next improvement project be that is related to HCISSP?
<--- Score

12. What are the key elements of your HCISSP performance improvement system, including

your evaluation, organizational learning, and innovation processes?
<--- Score

13. Is there a recommended audit plan for routine surveillance inspections of HCISSP's gains?
<--- Score

14. What is your quality control system?
<--- Score

15. Is reporting being used or needed?
<--- Score

16. What are we attempting to measure/monitor?
<--- Score

17. What other areas of the organization might benefit from the HCISSP team's improvements, knowledge, and learning?
<--- Score

18. What can you control?
<--- Score

19. What is your theory of human motivation, and how does your compensation plan fit with that view?
<--- Score

20. Were the planned controls in place?
<--- Score

21. Is a response plan established and deployed?
<--- Score

22. Does job training on the documented procedures

need to be part of the process team's education and training?
<--- Score

23. How will input, process, and output variables be checked to detect for sub-optimal conditions?
<--- Score

24. Is there a HCISSP Communication plan covering who needs to get what information when?
<--- Score

25. Will any special training be provided for results interpretation?
<--- Score

26. Are suggested corrective/restorative actions indicated on the response plan for known causes to problems that might surface?
<--- Score

27. If there currently is no plan, will a plan be developed?
<--- Score

28. Is a response plan in place for when the input, process, or output measures indicate an 'out-of-control' condition?
<--- Score

29. Were the planned controls working?
<--- Score

30. How will report readings be checked to effectively monitor performance?

<--- Score

31. Is new knowledge gained imbedded in the response plan?
<--- Score

32. Are operating procedures consistent?
<--- Score

33. In the case of a HCISSP project, the criteria for the audit derive from implementation objectives. an audit of a HCISSP project involves assessing whether the recommendations outlined for implementation have been met. in other words, can we track that any HCISSP project is implemented as planned, and is it working?
<--- Score

34. Is there a control plan in place for sustaining improvements (short and long-term)?
<--- Score

35. Implementation Planning- is a pilot needed to test the changes before a full roll out occurs?
<--- Score

36. Are there documented procedures?
<--- Score

37. How do our controls stack up?
<--- Score

38. Is there documentation that will support the successful operation of the improvement?
<--- Score

39. Who is the HCISSP process owner?
<--- Score

40. What are the known security controls?
<--- Score

41. What should we measure to verify effectiveness gains?
<--- Score

42. Are new process steps, standards, and documentation ingrained into normal operations?
<--- Score

43. Are controls in place and consistently applied?
<--- Score

44. How do you encourage people to take control and responsibility?
<--- Score

45. Who will be in control?
<--- Score

46. Do we monitor the HCISSP decisions made and fine tune them as they evolve?
<--- Score

47. Do the decisions we make today help people and the planet tomorrow?
<--- Score

48. What is the recommended frequency of auditing?
<--- Score

49. Do you monitor the effectiveness of your

HCISSP activities?
<--- Score

50. Does a troubleshooting guide exist or is it needed?
<--- Score

51. Does HCISSP appropriately measure and monitor risk?
<--- Score

52. Have new or revised work instructions resulted?
<--- Score

53. Whats the best design framework for HCISSP organization now that, in a post industrial-age if the top-down, command and control model is no longer relevant?
<--- Score

54. Has the improved process and its steps been standardized?
<--- Score

55. Who controls critical resources?
<--- Score

56. Is knowledge gained on process shared and institutionalized?
<--- Score

57. What other systems, operations, processes, and infrastructures (hiring practices, staffing, training, incentives/rewards, metrics/dashboards/scorecards, etc.) need updates, additions, changes, or deletions in order to facilitate knowledge transfer and improvements?

<--- Score

58. What should we measure to verify efficiency gains?
<--- Score

59. How will the process owner verify improvement in present and future sigma levels, process capabilities?
<--- Score

60. How will the day-to-day responsibilities for monitoring and continual improvement be transferred from the improvement team to the process owner?
<--- Score

61. What is our theory of human motivation, and how does our compensation plan fit with that view?
<--- Score

62. What key inputs and outputs are being measured on an ongoing basis?
<--- Score

63. Is there a standardized process?
<--- Score

64. What quality tools were useful in the control phase?
<--- Score

65. What is the control/monitoring plan?
<--- Score

66. What are your results for key measures or

indicators of the accomplishment of your HCISSP strategy and action plans, including building and strengthening core competencies?

<--- Score

67. Are pertinent alerts monitored, analyzed and distributed to appropriate personnel?

<--- Score

68. How do controls support value?

<--- Score

69. How might the organization capture best practices and lessons learned so as to leverage improvements across the business?

<--- Score

70. How likely is the current HCISSP plan to come in on schedule or on budget?

<--- Score

71. Do the HCISSP decisions we make today help people and the planet tomorrow?

<--- Score

72. Are documented procedures clear and easy to follow for the operators?

<--- Score

73. How do we enable market innovation while controlling security and privacy?

<--- Score

74. How will new or emerging customer needs/requirements be checked/communicated to orient the process toward meeting the new specifications

and continually reducing variation?
<--- Score

75. What are the critical parameters to watch?
<--- Score

76. Is there a transfer of ownership and knowledge to process owner and process team tasked with the responsibilities.
<--- Score

77. How does your workforce performance management system support high-performance work and workforce engagement; consider workforce compensation, reward, recognition, and incentive practices; and reinforce a customer and business focus and achievement of your action plans?
<--- Score

78. Will existing staff require re-training, for example, to learn new business processes?
<--- Score

Add up total points for this section:
_____ = Total points for this section

Divided by: _____ (number of statements answered) = _____
Average score for this section

Transfer your score to the HCISSP Index at the beginning of the Self-Assessment.

CRITERION #7: SUSTAIN:

INTENT: Retain the benefits.

In my belief, the answer to this question is clearly defined:

5 Strongly Agree

4 Agree

3 Neutral

2 Disagree

1 Strongly Disagree

1. Who are our customers?
<--- Score

2. Do you have an implicit bias for capital investments over people investments?
<--- Score

3. Were lessons learned captured and communicated?
<--- Score

4. What will drive HCISSP change?

<--- Score

5. What are the usability implications of HCISSP actions?
<--- Score

6. How does HCISSP integrate with other business initiatives?
<--- Score

7. What kind of crime could a potential new hire have committed that would not only not disqualify him/her from being hired by our organization, but would actually indicate that he/she might be a particularly good fit?
<--- Score

8. Which criteria are used to determine which projects are going to be pursued or discarded?
<--- Score

9. What management system can we use to leverage the HCISSP experience, ideas, and concerns of the people closest to the work to be done?
<--- Score

10. What am I trying to prove to myself, and how might it be hijacking my life and business success?
<--- Score

11. Who is responsible for errors?
<--- Score

12. What is our HCISSP Strategy?
<--- Score

13. What is the mission of the organization?
<--- Score

14. Whose voice (department, ethnic group, women, older workers, etc) might you have missed hearing from in your company, and how might you amplify this voice to create positive momentum for your business?
<--- Score

15. Did my employees make progress today?
<--- Score

16. How will we ensure we get what we expected?
<--- Score

17. Can we maintain our growth without detracting from the factors that have contributed to our success?
<--- Score

18. Do we think we know, or do we know we know ?
<--- Score

19. What do we do when new problems arise?
<--- Score

20. Who are you going to put out of business, and why?
<--- Score

21. Who are the key stakeholders?
<--- Score

22. Is the impact that HCISSP has shown?
<--- Score

23. What are the long-term HCISSP goals?
<--- Score

24. What have we done to protect our business from competitive encroachment?
<--- Score

25. Are we relevant? Will we be relevant five years from now? Ten?
<--- Score

26. How will we build a 100-year startup?
<--- Score

27. In the past year, what have you done (or could you have done) to increase the accurate perception of this company/brand as ethical and honest?
<--- Score

28. What trouble can we get into?
<--- Score

29. Are we paying enough attention to the partners our company depends on to succeed?
<--- Score

30. What potential megatrends could make our business model obsolete?
<--- Score

31. What are the rules and assumptions my industry operates under? What if the opposite were true?
<--- Score

32. How much contingency will be available in the budget?
<--- Score

33. Who do we think the world wants us to be?
<--- Score

34. What information is critical to our organization that our executives are ignoring?
<--- Score

35. What is it like to work for me?
<--- Score

36. What is our mission?
<--- Score

37. What may be the consequences for the performance of an organization if all stakeholders are not consulted regarding HCISSP?
<--- Score

38. Who will be responsible for deciding whether HCISSP goes ahead or not after the initial investigations?
<--- Score

39. How do we keep the momentum going?
<--- Score

40. What would I recommend my friend do if he were facing this dilemma?
<--- Score

41. If our customer were my grandmother, would I tell

her to buy what we're selling?
<--- Score

42. What trophy do we want on our mantle?
<--- Score

43. Are we making progress? and are we making progress as HCISSP leaders?
<--- Score

44. How Do We Create Buy-in?
<--- Score

45. Who do we want our customers to become?
<--- Score

46. How important is HCISSP to the user organizations mission?
<--- Score

47. Are there any disadvantages to implementing HCISSP? There might be some that are less obvious?
<--- Score

48. Is there any existing HCISSP governance structure?
<--- Score

49. Do we have enough freaky customers in our portfolio pushing us to the limit day in and day out?
<--- Score

50. What would have to be true for the option on the table to be the best possible choice?
<--- Score

51. Who, on the executive team or the board, has spoken to a customer recently?
<--- Score

52. What does your signature ensure?
<--- Score

53. Who is On the Team?
<--- Score

54. What principles do we value?
<--- Score

55. What are strategies for increasing support and reducing opposition?
<--- Score

56. How do we maintain HCISSP's Integrity?
<--- Score

57. What business benefits will HCISSP goals deliver if achieved?
<--- Score

58. Are we making progress?
<--- Score

59. Will there be any necessary staff changes (redundancies or new hires)?
<--- Score

60. Are we making progress (as leaders)?
<--- Score

61. Which models, tools and techniques are necessary?

<--- Score

62. Is a HCISSP Team Work effort in place?
<--- Score

63. How are we doing compared to our industry?
<--- Score

64. What did we miss in the interview for the worst hire we ever made?
<--- Score

65. What is the overall business strategy?
<--- Score

66. What happens when a new employee joins the organization?
<--- Score

67. Do your leaders set clear a direction that is aligned with the vision, mission, and values and is cascaded throughout the organization with measurable goals?
<--- Score

68. If our company went out of business tomorrow, would anyone who doesn't get a paycheck here care?
<--- Score

69. Would you rather sell to knowledgeable and informed customers or to uninformed customers?
<--- Score

70. What is our question?
<--- Score

71. What current systems have to be understood and/or changed?
<--- Score

72. How do we Lead with HCISSP in Mind?
<--- Score

73. You may have created your customer policies at a time when you lacked resources, technology wasn't up-to-snuff, or low service levels were the industry norm. Have those circumstances changed?
<--- Score

74. Who Uses What?
<--- Score

75. What are the critical success factors?
<--- Score

76. How will you know that the HCISSP project has been successful?
<--- Score

77. What are the gaps in my knowledge and experience?
<--- Score

78. How do we foster the skills, knowledge, talents, attributes, and characteristics we want to have?
<--- Score

79. Is there a lack of internal resources to do this work?
<--- Score

80. In retrospect, of the projects that we pulled the plug on, what percent do we wish had been allowed to keep going, and what percent do we wish had ended earlier?
<--- Score

81. What sources do you use to gather information for a HCISSP study?
<--- Score

82. Do we underestimate the customer's journey?
<--- Score

83. Do you have any supplemental information to add to this checklist?
<--- Score

84. Do we have the right capabilities and capacities?
<--- Score

85. How much does HCISSP help?
<--- Score

86. Have new benefits been realized?
<--- Score

87. Are we changing as fast as the world around us?
<--- Score

88. How do we ensure that implementations of HCISSP products are done in a way that ensures safety?
<--- Score

89. Is HCISSP dependent on the successful delivery of a current project?
<--- Score

90. Who sets the HCISSP standards?
<--- Score

91. What knowledge, skills and characteristics mark a good HCISSP project manager?
<--- Score

92. Instead of going to current contacts for new ideas, what if you reconnected with dormant contacts-- the people you used to know? If you were going reactivate a dormant tie, who would it be?
<--- Score

93. How are conflicts dealt with?
<--- Score

94. Are we / should we be Revolutionary or evolutionary?
<--- Score

95. What was the last experiment we ran?
<--- Score

96. How can you negotiate HCISSP successfully with a stubborn boss, an irate client, or a deceitful coworker?
<--- Score

97. Legal and contractual - are we allowed to do this?
<--- Score

98. If we got kicked out and the board brought in a

new CEO, what would he do?
<--- Score

99. Who will provide the final approval of HCISSP deliverables?
<--- Score

100. Do you have a vision statement?
<--- Score

101. What is the craziest thing we can do?
<--- Score

102. When information truly is ubiquitous, when reach and connectivity are completely global, when computing resources are infinite, and when a whole new set of impossibilities are not only possible, but happening, what will that do to our business?
<--- Score

103. How will we know when our strategy has been successful?
<--- Score

104. What is Effective HCISSP?
<--- Score

105. What are the challenges?
<--- Score

106. What is our formula for success in HCISSP ?
<--- Score

107. Do you see more potential in people than they do in themselves?
<--- Score

108. Is maximizing HCISSP protection the same as minimizing HCISSP loss?

<--- Score

109. Who is going to care?

<--- Score

110. How is business? Why?

<--- Score

111. If we weren't already in this business, would we enter it today? And if not, what are we going to do about it?

<--- Score

112. Do I know what I'm doing? And who do I call if I don't?

<--- Score

113. In a project to restructure HCISSP outcomes, which stakeholders would you involve?

<--- Score

114. Why are HCISSP skills important?

<--- Score

115. What is Tricky About This?

<--- Score

116. Who have we, as a company, historically been when we've been at our best?

<--- Score

117. How likely is it that a customer would recommend our company to a friend or colleague?

<--- Score

118. If I had to leave my organization for a year and the only communication I could have with employees was a single paragraph, what would I write?
<--- Score

119. Are you satisfied with your current role? If not, what is missing from it?
<--- Score

120. How do we accomplish our long range HCISSP goals?
<--- Score

121. What is a good product?
<--- Score

122. Ask yourself: how would we do this work if we only had one staff member to do it?
<--- Score

123. How do you govern and fulfill your societal responsibilities?
<--- Score

124. Is the HCISSP organization completing tasks effectively and efficiently?
<--- Score

125. If there were zero limitations, what would we do differently?
<--- Score

126. How can we become more high-tech but still be high touch?

<--- Score

127. Whom among your colleagues do you trust, and for what?

<--- Score

128. How can we incorporate support to ensure safe and effective use of HCISSP into the services that we provide?

<--- Score

129. Will it be accepted by users?

<--- Score

130. Is there any reason to believe the opposite of my current belief?

<--- Score

131. What new services of functionality will be implemented next with HCISSP ?

<--- Score

132. Are assumptions made in HCISSP stated explicitly?

<--- Score

133. Who uses our product in ways we never expected?

<--- Score

134. Is our strategy driving our strategy? Or is the way in which we allocate resources driving our strategy?

<--- Score

135. What threat is HCISSP addressing?

<--- Score

136. How do I stay inspired?
<--- Score

137. Do we say no to customers for no reason?
<--- Score

138. Why should people listen to you?
<--- Score

139. How would our PR, marketing, and social media change if we did not use outside agencies?
<--- Score

140. Schedule -can it be done in the given time?
<--- Score

141. What happens if you do not have enough funding?
<--- Score

142. How Do We Know if We Are Successful?
<--- Score

143. What is performance excellence?
<--- Score

144. What role does communication play in the success or failure of a HCISSP project?
<--- Score

145. How will we know if we have been successful?
<--- Score

146. Has implementation been effective in reaching specified objectives?

<--- Score

147. How do you determine the key elements that affect HCISSP workforce satisfaction? how are these elements determined for different workforce groups and segments?

<--- Score

148. What is your BATNA (best alternative to a negotiated agreement)?

<--- Score

149. What is the purpose of HCISSP in relation to the mission?

<--- Score

150. How do senior leaders set organizational vision and values?

<--- Score

151. What are our long-range and short-range goals?

<--- Score

152. We picked a method, now what?

<--- Score

153. What are the short and long-term HCISSP goals?

<--- Score

154. What one word do we want to own in the minds of our customers, employees, and partners?

<--- Score

155. How do senior leaders deploy your

organizations vision and values through your leadership system, to the workforce, to key suppliers and partners, and to customers and other stakeholders, as appropriate?

<--- Score

156. Are the criteria for selecting recommendations stated?

<--- Score

157. How long will it take to change?

<--- Score

158. Which functions and people interact with the supplier and or customer?

<--- Score

159. Am I failing differently each time?

<--- Score

160. What are your organizations work systems?

<--- Score

161. Where is our petri dish?

<--- Score

162. What is a feasible sequencing of reform initiatives over time?

<--- Score

163. What are we challenging, in the sense that Mac challenged the PC or Dove tackled the Beauty Myth?

<--- Score

164. How do we manage HCISSP Knowledge Management (KM)?

<--- Score

165. Are new benefits received and understood?
<--- Score

166. What are specific HCISSP Rules to follow?
<--- Score

167. Who is the main stakeholder, with ultimate responsibility for driving HCISSP forward?
<--- Score

168. Where is your organization on the performance excellence continuum?
<--- Score

169. Have benefits been optimized with all key stakeholders?
<--- Score

170. Why don't our customers like us?
<--- Score

171. What is our competitive advantage?
<--- Score

172. Has the investment re-baselined during the past fiscal year?
<--- Score

173. Have totally satisfied customers?
<--- Score

174. Political -is anyone trying to undermine this project?
<--- Score

175. How do we foster innovation?

<--- Score

176. Who is responsible for ensuring appropriate resources (time, people and money) are allocated to HCISSP?
<--- Score

177. What stupid rule would we most like to kill?
<--- Score

178. Who else should we help?

<--- Score

179. What are the business goals HCISSP is aiming to achieve?
<--- Score

180. How to deal with HCISSP Changes?
<--- Score

181. If we do not follow, then how to lead?

<--- Score

182. How to Secure HCISSP?
<--- Score

183. Are the assumptions believable and achievable?

<--- Score

184. Do we have the right people on the bus?
<--- Score

185. Will I get fired?

<--- Score

186. Do HCISSP rules make a reasonable demand on a users capabilities?
<--- Score

187. What is the estimated value of the project?
<--- Score

188. To whom do you add value?
<--- Score

189. How will we insure seamless interoperability of HCISSP moving forward?
<--- Score

190. Who will use it?
<--- Score

191. What are the Essentials of Internal HCISSP Management?
<--- Score

192. How do we go about Securing HCISSP?
<--- Score

193. What are the success criteria that will indicate that HCISSP objectives have been met and the benefits delivered?
<--- Score

194. Among our stronger employees, how many see themselves at the company in three years? How many would leave for a 10 percent raise from another company?
<--- Score

195. If no one would ever find out about my accomplishments, how would I lead differently?
<--- Score

196. How do we engage the workforce, in addition to satisfying them?
<--- Score

197. Do you keep 50% of your time unscheduled?
<--- Score

198. Who will determine interim and final deadlines?
<--- Score

199. What will be the consequences to the stakeholder (financial, reputation etc) if HCISSP does not go ahead or fails to deliver the objectives?
<--- Score

200. What is the range of capabilities?
<--- Score

201. What is an unauthorized commitment?
<--- Score

202. Operational - will it work?
<--- Score

203. Is it economical; do we have the time and money?
<--- Score

204. Who will manage the integration of tools?
<--- Score

205. What external factors influence our success?
<--- Score

206. If you had to rebuild your organization without any traditional competitive advantages (i.e., no killer a technology, promising research, innovative product/service delivery model, etc.), how would your people have to approach their work and collaborate together in order to create the necessary conditions for success?
<--- Score

207. Which individuals, teams or departments will be involved in HCISSP?
<--- Score

208. Why should we adopt a HCISSP framework?
<--- Score

209. How do you listen to customers to obtain actionable information?
<--- Score

210. Have highly satisfied employees?
<--- Score

211. How do we make it meaningful in connecting HCISSP with what users do day-to-day?
<--- Score

212. What counts that we are not counting?
<--- Score

213. Think about the kind of project structure that would be appropriate for your HCISSP project.

should it be formal and complex, or can it be less formal and relatively simple?
<--- Score

214. How can we become the company that would put us out of business?
<--- Score

215. What is the funding source for this project?
<--- Score

216. How do we provide a safe environment -physically and emotionally?
<--- Score

217. If you were responsible for initiating and implementing major changes in your organization, what steps might you take to ensure acceptance of those changes?
<--- Score

218. What are your key business, operational, societal responsibility, and human resource strategic challenges and advantages?
<--- Score

219. What are internal and external HCISSP relations?
<--- Score

220. Think of your HCISSP project. what are the main functions?
<--- Score

221. What happens at this company when people fail?
<--- Score

222. Marketing budgets are tighter, consumers are more skeptical, and social media has changed forever the way we talk about HCISSP. How do we gain traction?
<--- Score

223. What should we stop doing?
<--- Score

224. Are there HCISSP Models?
<--- Score

225. In what ways are HCISSP vendors and us interacting to ensure safe and effective use?
<--- Score

226. Who are four people whose careers I've enhanced?
<--- Score

227. What is something you believe that nearly no one agrees with you on?
<--- Score

228. Where can we break convention?
<--- Score

229. Which HCISSP goals are the most important?
<--- Score

230. What are all of our HCISSP domains and what do they do?
<--- Score

231. What are your most important goals for the strategic HCISSP objectives?

<--- Score

232. But does it really, really work?
<--- Score

Add up total points for this section:
_____ = Total points for this section

Divided by: _____ (number of statements answered) = _____
Average score for this section

Transfer your score to the HCISSP Index at the beginning of the Self-Assessment.

HCISSP and Managing HCISSP Projects, Criteria for HCISSP Project Managers:

HCISSP: Planning Process Group

1. How are IT HCISSP Projects different?

2. Contingency planning. If a risk event occurs, what will you do?

3. How can you tell when you are done?

4. What factors are contributing to progress or delay in the achievement of products and results?

5. Is the pace of implementing the products of the programme ensuring the completeness of the results of the HCISSP Project?

6. How does activity resource estimation affect activity duration estimation?

7. What input will you be required to provide the HCISSP Project team?

8. You did your readings, yes?

9. Why is it important to determine activity sequencing on HCISSP Projects?

10. What types of differentiated effects are resulting from the HCISSP Project and to what extent?

11. In what ways can the governance of the HCISSP Project be improved so that it has greater likelihood of achieving future sustainability?

12. What will you do to minimize the impact should a

risk event occur?

13. To what extent are the visions and actions of the partners consistent or divergent with regard to the program?

14. Just how important is your work to the overall success of the HCISSP Project?

15. How can you make your needs known?

16. Are work methodologies, financial instruments, etc. shared among departments, organizations and HCISSP Projects?

17. In what way has the HCISSP Project come up with innovative measures for problem-solving?

18. The HCISSP Project Charter is created in which HCISSP Project management process group?

19. How will it affect you?

20. When developing the estimates for HCISSP Project phases, you choose to add the individual estimates for the activities that comprise each phase. What type of estimation method are you using?

HCISSP: Cost Management Plan

21. For cost control purposes?

22. Are internal HCISSP Project status meetings held at reasonable intervals?

23. Are the schedule estimates reasonable given the HCISSP Project?

24. Are the payment terms being followed?

25. Are the results of quality assurance reviews provided to affected groups & individuals?

26. Have key stakeholders been identified?

27. Milestones – What are the key dates in executing the contract plan?

28. Published materials?

29. Exclusions – Is there scope to be performed or provided by others?

30. Are milestone deliverables effectively tracked and compared to HCISSP Project plan?

31. Has the budget been baselined?

32. Is a PMO (HCISSP Project Management Office) in place and provide oversight to the HCISSP Project?

33. Quality Assurance overheads?

34. Were stakeholders aware and supportive of the principles and practices of modern software estimation?

35. Resources – How will human resources be scheduled during each phase of the HCISSP Project?

36. Sensitivity analysis?

37. Have all team members been part of identifying risks?

38. Has a Quality Assurance Plan been developed for the HCISSP Project?

39. Responsibilities – What is the split of responsibilities between the owner and contractors?

40. Schedule contingency – How will the schedule contingency be administrated?

HCISSP: Quality Metrics

41. When is the security analysis testing complete?

42. What if the biggest risk to your business were those people who dont complain?

43. If the defect rate during testing is substantially higher than that of the previous release (or a similar product), then ask: Did you plan for and actually improve testing effectiveness?

44. Has trace of defects been initiated?

45. What makes a visualization memorable?

46. Product Availability ?

47. There are many reasons to shore up quality-related metrics, but what metrics are important?

48. What are the organizations expectations for its quality HCISSP Project?

49. Are quality metrics defined?

50. Is material complete (and does it meet the standards)?

51. Which data do others need in one place to target areas of improvement?

52. Do the operators focus on determining; is there anything I need to worry about?

53. What happens if you get an abnormal result?

54. Where is Quality Now?

55. What metrics do you measure?

56. What is the benchmark?

57. Did evaluation start on time?

58. How does one achieve stability?

59. Is the reporting frequency appropriate?

60. What does this tell us?

HCISSP: Team Member Status Report

61. Does the organization have the means (staff, money, contract, etc.) to produce or to acquire the product, good, or service?

62. Do you have an Enterprise HCISSP Project Management Office (EPMO)?

63. How will Resource Planning be done?

64. How does this product, good, or service meet the needs of the HCISSP Project and the organization as a whole?

65. Does every department have to have a HCISSP Project Manager on staff?

66. What is to be done?

67. How much risk is involved?

68. What specific interest groups do you have in place?

69. Are the products of the organization's HCISSP Projects meeting their customer's objectives?

70. The problem with Reward & Recognition Programs is that the truly deserving people all too often get left out. How can you make it practical?

71. Is there evidence that staff is taking a more professional approach toward management of the

organizations HCISSP Projects?

72. Why is it to be done?

73. How can you make it practical?

74. How it is to be done?

75. Are the attitudes of staff regarding HCISSP Project work improving?

76. Are the organization's HCISSP Projects more successful over time?

77. Does the product, good, or service already exist within the organization?

78. When a teams productivity and success depend on collaboration and the efficient flow of information, what generally fails them?

79. Will the staff do training or is that done by a third party?

HCISSP: Human Resource Management Plan

80. How will the HCISSP Project manage expectations & meet needs and requirements?

81. Who will be impacted (both positively and negatively) as a result of or during the execution of this HCISSP Project?

82. Responsiveness to change and the resulting demands for different skills and abilities?

83. How do you determine what key skills and talents are needed to meet the objectives. Is the company primarily focused on a specific industry?

84. Are parking lot items captured?

85. Cost / Benefit Analysis?

86. Based on your HCISSP Project communication management plan, what worked well?

87. Are key risk mitigation strategies added to the HCISSP Project schedule?

88. Is there general agreement & acceptance of the current status and progress of the HCISSP Project?

89. Is there an onboarding process in place?

90. Are Vendor invoices audited for accuracy before

payment?

91. Is the manpower level sufficient to meet the future business requirements?

92. Measurable - Are the targets measurable?

93. Explain the purpose of this HCISSP Project by describing, at a high-level, what will be done. What is this HCISSP Project aiming to achieve?

94. Is there a Quality Management Plan?

95. Have the key elements of a coherent HCISSP Project management strategy been established?

96. Does a documented HCISSP Project organizational policy & plan (i.e. governance model) exist?

97. Are the right people being attracted and retained to meet the future challenges?

HCISSP: Work Breakdown Structure

98. How Far Down?

99. When would you develop a Work Breakdown Structure?

100. How will you and your HCISSP Project team define the HCISSP Projects scope and work breakdown structure?

101. Can you make it?

102. How many levels?

103. What is the probability that the HCISSP Project duration will exceed xx weeks?

104. Why would you develop a Work Breakdown Structure?

105. When does it have to be done?

106. Is it still viable?

107. How big is a work-package?

108. Is it a change in scope?

109. Is the Work breakdown Structure (WBS) defined and is the scope of the HCISSP Project clear with assigned deliverable owners?

110. How much detail?

111. Do you need another level?

112. What is the probability of completing the HCISSP Project in less that xx days?

113. Where does it take place?

114. Why is it useful?

115. What has to be done?

116. Who has to do it?

117. When do you stop?

HCISSP: HCISSP Project Portfolio management

118. The portfolio management process force ranks work based on known strategic direction; What do you want to achieve strategically for the current and subsequent fiscal years?

119. Why would the Governance Board want to know the status of the resource portfolio?

120. Agility. How do organizations re-align portfolio when strategic objectives change?

121. When starting a new PMO, what are the steps that need to be taken to have a final resource portfolio?

122. What are the four types of portfolios a PMO must focus on?

123. Are portfolios aligned to strategic business objectives?

124. Why would the Governance Board want to know the current portfolio opportunity?

125. Regularly review and revise the HCISSP Project portfolio (eg several times a year) are done?

126. Strategic fit. Are portfolios aligned to strategic business objectives?

127. What Happens without HCISSP Project Portfolio and Proper Resourcing?

128. What are the biggest dos and donts for the PMO to consider when performing resource portfolio management?

129. What is a right HCISSP Project portfolio?

130. How does the organization ensure that HCISSP Project and program benefits and risks are being managed to optimize the overall value creation from the portfolio?

131. What is HCISSP Project portfolio management?

132. How do organizations re-align portfolio when strategic objectives change?

133. How much information about an asset do you think a PMO needs to develop its asset portfolio?

134. Why is HCISSP Project portfolio management (PPM) important?

135. Do you have a risk-based approach to portfolio management?

136. Why is implementation of resource portfolio management recommended in the last stage?

137. What is the meaning of balancing a portfolio?

HCISSP: Milestone List

138. What is the market for your technology, product or service?

139. Marketing - reach, distribution, awareness?

140. Milestone pages should display the UserID of the person who added the milestone. Does a report or query exist that provides this audit information?

141. Reliability of data, plan predictability?

142. Describe the concept of the technology, product or service that will be or has been developed. How will it be used?

143. How difficult will it be to do specific activities on this HCISSP Project?

144. Environmental effects?

145. New USPs?

146. How soon can the activity finish?

147. What date will the task finish?

148. Continuity, supply chain robustness?

149. Describe the companys strengths and core competencies. What factors will make the company succeed?

150. Calculate how long can activity be delayed?

151. Global influences?

152. How Do you Manage Time?

153. Are the required resources available or need to be acquired?

154. How late can the activity finish?

155. How will you get the word out to customers?

156. Timescales, deadlines and pressures?

157. Gaps in capabilities?

HCISSP: Lessons Learned

158. How satisfied are you with your involvement in the development and/or review of the HCISSP Project Scope during HCISSP Project Initiation and Planning?

159. How effective were HCISSP Project audits?

160. How timely were Progress Reports provided to the HCISSP Project Manager by Team Members?

161. How effective were the communications materials in providing and orienting team members about the details of the HCISSP Project?

162. How well does the product or service the HCISSP Project produced meet your needs?

163. How well did the scope of the HCISSP Project match what was defined in the HCISSP Project Proposal?

164. How efficient were HCISSP Project team meetings conducted?

165. How well does the product or service the HCISSP Project produced meet the defined HCISSP Project requirements?

166. How effective were Best Practices & Lessons Learned from prior HCISSP Projects utilized in this HCISSP Project?

167. Was HCISSP Project performance validated or

challenged?

168. What is your overall assessment of the outcome of this HCISSP Project?

169. How did the estimated HCISSP Project Budget compare with the total actual expenditures?

HCISSP: Risk Register

170. Do you require further engagement?

171. When will it happen?

172. What is our current and future risk profile?

173. What Went Wrong?

174. Are there any knock-on effects/impact on any of the other areas?

175. How often will the Risk Management Plan and Risk Register be formally reviewed, and by whom?

176. Financial risk -can the organization afford to undertake the HCISSP Project?

177. Why would you develop a risk register?

178. Market risk -Will the new service or product be useful to the organization or marketable to others?

179. Are corrective measures implemented as planned?

180. What could prevent us delivering on the strategic program objectives and what is being done to mitigate such issues?

181. Cost/Benefit – How much will the proposed mitigations cost and how does this cost compare with the potential cost of the risk event/situation should it

occur?

182. What action, if any, has been taken to respond to the risk?

183. How are Risks Identified?

184. What should you do when?

185. How is a Community Risk Register created?

186. How well are risks controlled?

187. What is the reason for current performance gaps and do the risks and opportunities identified previously explain this?

188. Does the evidence highlight any areas to advance opportunities or foster good relations. If yes what steps will be taken?

189. Manageability – Have mitigations to the risk been identified?

HCISSP: Stakeholder Management Plan

190. How are you doing/what can be done better?

191. Are procurement deliverables arriving on time and to specification?

192. How will you engage this stakeholder and gain their commitment?

193. Who might be involved in developing a charter?

194. What records are required (eg purchase orders, agreements)?

195. Where to Get Additional Help?

196. Is there a requirements change management processes in place?

197. Is there an issues management plan in place?

198. Has the HCISSP Project manager been identified?

199. How accurate and complete is the information?

200. Are estimating assumptions and constraints captured?

201. Does the HCISSP Project have a formal HCISSP Project Plan?

202. Are individual tasks of reasonable time effort (8–40 hours)?

203. Have HCISSP Project success criteria been defined?

204. Are post milestone HCISSP Project reviews (PMPR) conducted with the organization at least once a year?

205. Are all resource assumptions documented?

206. Are all Vendor contracts are closed out?

207. What has to be purchased?

208. How are stakeholders chosen and what roles might they have on a HCISSP Project?

209. Do any protocols apply for records management?

HCISSP: Activity Duration Estimates

210. What is the organizations history in doing similar activities?

211. What are some of the options you found to help people prepare for the exam?

212. Are updates on work results collected and used as inputs to the performance reporting process?

213. A HCISSP Project has three critical paths. Which BEST describes how this affects the HCISSP Project?

214. Who will promote it?

215. Under these circumstances what would be the best thing to do?

216. Can they use those?

217. What functions does this software provide that cannot be done easily using other tools such as a spreadsheet or database?

218. On which process should team members spend the most time?

219. Does a process exist to identify individuals authorized to make certain decisions?

220. Does a process exist to identify HCISSP Project roles, responsibilities and reporting relationships?

221. Which frame seemed to be the most important and why?

222. Where Do Schedules Come From?

223. Will new hardware or software be required for servers or client machines?

224. What are some of the HCISSP Project management deliverables of each process group?

225. Is earned value analysis completed to assess HCISSP Project performance?

226. Is evaluation criteria defined to rate proposals?

227. What is the shortest possible time it will take to complete this HCISSP Project?

HCISSP: Team Performance Assessment

228. To what degree are the goals ambitious?

229. Delaying Market Entry: How Long Is too Long?

230. Where to from here?

231. What is method variance?

232. What are Teams?

233. How Do you Manage Human Resources?

234. When does the medium matter?

235. Can familiarity breed backup?

236. To what degree are the goals realistic?

HCISSP: Risk Data Sheet

237. What will be the consequences if it happens?

238. What are you trying to achieve (Objectives)?

239. Are new hazards created?

240. What Do you Know?

241. Potential for Recurrence?

242. Will revised controls lead to tolerable risk levels?

243. What is the likelihood of it happening?

244. Would you prefer an unknown or 70/30 chance?

245. How can hazards be reduced?

246. What is the chance that it will happen?

247. What was Measured?

248. Type of Risk Identified?

249. What is the environment within which you operate (social trends, economic, community values, broad based participation, national directions etc.)?

250. What can happen?

251. What are the main threats to our existence?

252. Is the data sufficiently specified in terms of the type of failure being analysed, and its frequency or probability?

253. During work activities could hazards exist?

254. How do you handle product safely?

255. Whom do you serve (customers)?

256. What is the duration of infection (the length of time the host is infected with the organism) in a normal healthy human host?

HCISSP: Network Diagram

257. What can be done concurrently?

258. Are the required resources available?

259. What are the Major Administrative Issues?

260. Exercise: What is the probability that the HCISSP Project duration will exceed xx weeks?

261. What activities must occur simultaneously with this activity?

262. What must be completed before an activity can be started?

263. Are the Gantt Chart and/or Network Diagram updated periodically and used to assess the overall HCISSP Project timetable?

264. What job or jobs follow it?

265. Which type of network diagram allows you to depict four types of dependencies?

266. Planning: who, how long, what to do?

267. What is the lowest cost to complete this HCISSP Project in xx weeks?

268. Are you on time?

269. What job or jobs could run concurrently?

270. If X is long, what would be the completion time if you break X into two parallel parts of y weeks and z weeks?

271. What activity must be completed immediately before this activity can start?

272. How confident can you be in our milestone dates and the delivery date?

273. Will crashing x weeks return more in benefits than it costs?

274. What to do and When?

HCISSP: Procurement Audit

275. Is there a legal authority for the procurement HCISSP Project?

276. Has alternatives been considered for the specified procurement HCISSP Project?

277. Has the expected benefits from realisation of the procurement HCISSP Project been calculated?

278. Does the procurement HCISSP Project have a clear goal and does the goal meet the specified needs of the users?

279. Is the procurement HCISSP Project efficiently managed?

280. Is the foreseen budget compared with similar HCISSP Projects or procurements yet realised (historical standards)?

281. Is there a need for the procurement HCISSP Project at all?

282. Are there appropriate controls in place to ensure that the procurement HCISSP Project complies with relevant legislation?

283. Does the procurement HCISSP Project comply with European Communities regulations and rules?

HCISSP: Team Directory

284. Where will the product be used and/or delivered or built when appropriate?

285. When will you produce deliverables?

286. Process Decisions: Do job conditions warrant additional actions to collect job information and document on-site activity?

287. Process Decisions: Is work progressing on schedule and per contract requirements?

288. Process Decisions: How well was task order work performed?

289. Contract requirements complied with?

290. Who will write the meeting minutes and distribute?

291. How will you accomplish and manage the objectives?

292. Who will talk to the customer?

293. Decisions: Is the most suitable form of contract being used?

294. Who is the Sponsor?

295. Do purchase specifications and configurations match requirements?

296. Decisions: What could be done better to improve the quality of the constructed product?

297. Who are the stakeholders?

298. Who are your stakeholders (customers, sponsors, end users, team members)?

299. How will the team handle changes?

300. Is construction on schedule?

301. Process Decisions: Are there any statutory or regulatory issues relevant to the timely execution of work?

302. Who will report HCISSP Project status to all stakeholders?

303. Process Decisions: Which organizational elements and which individuals will be assigned management functions?

HCISSP: Executing Process Group

304. What are the main types of contracts if you do decide to outsource?

305. Would you rate yourself as being risk-averse, risk-neutral, or risk-seeking?

306. What does it mean to take a systems view of a HCISSP Project?

307. Do the partners have sufficient financial capacity to keep up the benefits produced by the programme?

308. What are some crucial elements of a good HCISSP Project plan?

309. What are deliverables of your HCISSP Project?

310. How Will You Know You Did It?

311. Are decisions made in a timely manner?

312. What type of information goes in the quality assurance plan?

313. What are crucial elements of successful HCISSP Project plan execution?

314. Who will provide training?

315. Does the HCISSP Project team have the right skills?

316. What type of people would you want on your team?

317. What Business Situation Is Being Addressed?

318. Will outside resources be needed to help?

319. Is the HCISSP Project performing better or worse than planned?

320. Does the HCISSP Project team have enough people to execute the HCISSP Project plan?

321. In what way has the programme come up with innovative measures for problem-solving?

322. What were things that you need to improve?

HCISSP: Stakeholder Analysis Matrix

323. How do rules, behaviors affect stakes?

324. Who has not been involved up to now but should have been?

325. How will the stakeholder directly benefit from the HCISSP Project and how will this affect the stakeholders motivation?

326. How much do resources cost?

327. Benefit to whom?

328. Competitive advantages?

329. What is the stakeholders power and status in relation to the HCISSP Project?

330. Inoculations or payment to receive them?

331. Why do you need to manage HCISSP Project Risk?

332. Disadvantages of proposition?

333. What is their relationship with the HCISSP Project?

334. What is the relationship among stakeholders?

335. What do the orgabizations stakeholders do better than anyone else?

336. Who has been involved in the area (thematic or geographic) in the past?

337. Who is most dependent on the resources at stake?

338. Whats the stakeholder's name, whats their function?

339. Location and geographical?

340. What obstacles does the organization face?

341. Who holds positions of responsibility in interested organizations?

342. Do any safeguard policies apply to the HCISSP Project?

HCISSP: Communications Management Plan

343. Are there potential barriers between the team and the stakeholder?

344. Who is involved as you identify stakeholders?

345. How Do you Manage Communications?

346. Who are the members of the governing body?

347. Who were proponents/opponents?

348. Which team member will work with each stakeholder?

349. What to know?

350. How is this initiative related to other portfolios, programs, or HCISSP Projects?

351. Can you think of other people who might have concerns or interests?

352. What Went Right?

353. What steps can you take for a positive relationship?

354. How will the person responsible for executing the communication item be notified?

355. How much time does it take to do it?

356. Are there too many who have an interest in some aspect of your work?

357. What communications method?

358. Are others part of the communications management plan?

359. What help do you and your team need from the stakeholder?

360. Which stakeholders are thought leaders, influences, or early adopters?

361. How were such initiatives successful?

HCISSP: Assumption and Constraint Log

362. Were the system requirements formally reviewed prior to initiating the design phase?

363. Would known impacts serve as impediments?

364. Are processes for release management of new development from coding and unit testing, to integration testing, to training, and production defined and followed?

365. Violation Trace: Why ?

366. Are there standards for code development?

367. Are there processes in place to ensure internal consistency between the source code components?

368. Is the Steering Committee active in HCISSP Project oversight?

369. Are there cosmetic errors that hinder readability and comprehension?

370. Do documented requirements exist for all critical components and areas, including technical, business, interfaces, performance, security and conversion requirements?

371. Is the current scope of the HCISSP Project substantially different than that originally defined in

the approved HCISSP Project plan?

372. What if failure during recovery?

373. Is the amount of effort justified by the anticipated value of forming a new process?

374. Has a HCISSP Project Communications Plan been developed?

375. Does the Plan conform to standards?

376. What other teams / processes would be impacted by changes to the current process, and how?

377. Contradictory information between different documents?

378. Do you know what our customers expectations are regarding this process?

379. Have the scope, objectives, costs, benefits and impacts been communicated to all involved and/or impacted stakeholders and work groups?

380. What Threats might prevent us from getting there?

HCISSP: Roles and Responsibilities

381. Does the team have access to and ability to use data analysis tools?

382. Are HCISSP Project team roles and responsibilities identified and documented?

383. Was the expectation clearly communicated?

384. Whats working well?

385. Are the quality assurance functions and related roles and responsibilities clearly defined?

386. Implementation of actions: Who are the responsible units?

387. How well did the HCISSP Project Team understand the expectations of specific roles and responsibilities?

388. Is there a training program in place for stakeholders covering expectations, roles and responsibilities and any addition knowledge others need to be good stakeholders?

389. Are governance roles and responsibilities documented?

390. What should you do now to ensure that you are exceeding expectations and excelling in your current position?

391. What expectations were NOT met?

392. Attainable / Achievable: The goal is attainable; can you actually accomplish the goal?

393. What should you do now to prepare yourself for a promotion, increased responsibilities or a different job?

394. Key conclusions and recommendations: Are conclusions and recommendations relevant and acceptable?

395. What expectations were met?

396. Are our budgets supportive of a culture of quality data?

397. What areas would you highlight for changes or improvements?

398. Where are you most strong as a supervisor?

399. What should you do now to prepare for your career 5+ years from now?

400. Concern: where are you limited or have no authority, where you cant influence?

HCISSP: Formal Acceptance

401. Did the HCISSP Project achieve its MOV?

402. General estimate of the costs and times do complete the HCISSP Project. (Answers the question: Is this a peanut or an elephant?

403. Was the HCISSP Project managed well?

404. Is formal acceptance of the HCISSP Project product documented and distributed?

405. Was the client satisfied with the HCISSP Project results?

406. What lessons were learned about your HCISSP Project management methodology?

407. Was the HCISSP Project work done on time, within budget, and according to specification?

408. How does your team plan to obtain formal acceptance on your HCISSP Project?

409. Does it do what HCISSP Project team said it would?

410. Did the HCISSP Project manager and team act in a professional and ethical manner?

411. Was the HCISSP Project goal achieved?

HCISSP: Quality Audit

412. How does the organization know whether they are adhering to their mission and achieving their objectives?

413. How does the organization know that its relationships with industry and employers are appropriately effective and constructive?

414. Statements of intent remain exactly that until they are put into effect. The next step is to deploy those intentions. In other words, do the plans happen in reality?

415. How does your organization ensure that equipment is appropriately maintained and producing valid results?

416. How does the organization know that its relationship with its (past) staff is appropriately effective and constructive?

417. Are the intentions consistent with external obligations (such as applicable laws)?

418. What review processes are in place for the organizations major activities?

419. Is there any content that may be legally actionable?

420. How does the organization know that its management of its ethical responsibilities is

appropriately effective and constructive?

421. Are there appropriate means for intervening if necessary?

422. How does the organization know that the support for its staff is appropriately effective and constructive?

423. How does the organization know that its Strategic Plan is providing the best guidance for the future of the organization?

424. How does the organization know that its system for commercializing research outputs is appropriately effective and constructive?

425. How does the organization know that its system for ensuring that its training activities are appropriately resourced and support is appropriately effective and constructive?

426. Are multiple statements on the same issue consistent with each other?

427. How does the organization know that its staff are presenting original work, and properly acknowledging the work of others?

428. Do all staff have the necessary authority and resources to deliver what is expected of them?

429. How does the organization know that its system for recruiting the best staff possible are appropriately effective and constructive?

430. How does the organization know that its systems for communicating with and among staff are appropriately effective and constructive?

431. Can the organization demonstrate exactly how and why results were achieved?

HCISSP: Requirements Management Plan

432. Describe the process for rejecting the HCISSP Project requirements. Who has the authority to reject HCISSP Project requirements?

433. Do you have an agreed upon process for alerting the HCISSP Project Manager if a request for change in requirements leads to a product scope change?

434. Did you distinguish the scope of work the contractor(s) will be required to do?

435. Will you document changes to requirements?

436. Did you provide clear and concise specifications?

437. How knowledgeable is the team in the proposed application area?

438. The WBS is developed as part of a Joint Planning session. But how do you know that youve done this right?

439. Will you use an assessment of the HCISSP Project environment as a tool to discover risk to the requirements process?

440. Are all the stakeholders ready for the transition into the user community?

441. Who will finally present the work or product(s) for

acceptance?

442. Is the system software (non-operating system) new to the IT HCISSP Project team?

443. Did you avoid subjective, flowery or non-specific statements?

444. How do you know that you have done this right?

445. Do you understand the role that each stakeholder will play in the requirements process?

446. What is the earliest finish date for this HCISSP Project if it is scheduled to start on ...?

447. Will the product release be stable and mature enough to be deployed in the user community?

448. Business analysis scope?

449. Define the Help Desk model. Who will take full responsibility?

HCISSP: Risk Management Plan

450. Does the software engineering team have the right mix of skills?

451. What does a risk management program do?

452. Are people attending meetings and doing work?

453. Are the software tools integrated with each other?

454. Which risks should get the attention?

455. How well were you able to manage your risk before?

456. Minimize cost and financial risk?

457. Have top software and customer managers formally committed to support the HCISSP Project?

458. How would you suggest monitoring for risk transition indicators?

459. People risk -Are people with appropriate skills available to help complete the HCISSP Project?

460. For software; Does the software interface with new or unproven hardware or unproven vendor products?

461. Why might it be late?

462. What did not work so well?

463. Do the requirements require the creation of components that are unlike anything your organization has previously built?

464. Who/what Can Assist?

465. Is HCISSP Project scope stable?

466. What are the cost, schedule and resource impacts of avoiding the risk?

467. Anticipated volatility of the requirements?

468. Does the HCISSP Project team have experience with the technology to be implemented?

HCISSP: Closing Process Group

469. What level of risk does the proposed budget represent to the HCISSP Project?

470. Is this a follow-on to a previous HCISSP Project?

471. How critical is the HCISSP Project success to the success of the organization?

472. How well defined and documented were the HCISSP Project management processes you chose to use?

473. What is the HCISSP Project name and date of completion?

474. How Well Did You Do?

475. Will the HCISSP Project deliverable(s) replace a current asset or group of assets?

476. Is the HCISSP Project Funded?

477. When will the HCISSP Project be done?

478. Did the HCISSP Project team have enough people to execute the HCISSP Project plan?

479. Did the HCISSP Project management methodology work?

480. How well did the chosen processes fit the needs of the HCISSP Project?

481. What is the amount of funding and what HCISSP Project phases are funded?

482. How Will You Do It?

483. Did the delivered product meet the specified requirements and goals of the HCISSP Project?

484. What Will You Do?

485. What is the overall risk of the HCISSP Project to the organization?

486. What areas does the group agree are the biggest success on the HCISSP Project?

HCISSP: Activity Cost Estimates

487. What is HCISSP Project Cost Management?

488. Will you need to provide essential services information about activities?

489. Would you hire them again?

490. How and when do you enter into HCISSP Project Procurement Management?

491. Does the activity rely on a common set of tools to carry it out?

492. Were decisions made in a timely manner?

493. Is costing method consistent with study goals?

494. Why Do you Manage Cost?

495. Scope statement only direct or indirect costs as well?

496. How do you do activity recasts?

497. What is the last item a HCISSP Project manager must do to finalize HCISSP Project close-out?

498. The impact and what actions were taken?

499. Are cost subtotals needed?

500. Does the activity use a common approach or

business function to deliver its results?

501. Can you change our activities?

502. Who & what determines the need for contracted services?

503. What is the activity inventory?

504. How Award?

HCISSP: Requirements Documentation

505. What is the risk associated with the technology?

506. Is the requirement properly understood?

507. How linear / iterative is your Requirements Gathering process (or will it be)?

508. How will they be documented / shared?

509. Is the origin of the requirement clearly stated?

510. Verifiability. Can the requirements be checked?

511. How will Requirements be documented and who signs off on them?

512. What will be the integration problems?

513. Are there any requirements conflicts?

514. How does what is being described meet the business need?

515. Can the requirements be checked?

516. Have the benefits identified with the system being identified clearly?

517. Basic work/Business process; high-level, what is being touched?

518. What Can Tools Do For Us?

519. What images does it conjure?

520. Is your Business Case still valid?

521. What if the system wasn t implemented?

522. Completeness. Are all functions required by the customer included?

523. Is the requirement realistically testable?

524. Who is involved?

HCISSP: Activity Resource Requirements

525. How many signatures do you require on a check and does this match what is in your policy and procedures?

526. Are there unresolved issues that need to be addressed?

527. Anything else?

528. What is the Work Plan Standard?

529. When does Monitoring Begin?

530. Which logical relationship does the PDM use most often?

531. How do you handle petty cash?

532. Why do you do that?

533. Is there anything planned that doesn t need to be here?

534. What are constraints that you might find during the Human Resource Planning process?

535. Other support in specific areas?

536. Time for overtime?

537. Do you use tools like decomposition and rolling-wave planning to produce the activity list and other outputs?

538. Organizational Applicability?

HCISSP: HCISSP Project Scope Statement

539. Is the HCISSP Project Sponsor function identified and defined?

540. Are the input requirements from the team members clearly documented and communicated?

541. Will the Risk Plan be updated on a regular and frequent basis?

542. Has the HCISSP Project Scope Statement been reviewed as part of the baseline process?

543. Will the Risk Status be reported to management on a regular and frequent basis?

544. Will the HCISSP Project risks being managed be according to the HCISSP Projects risk management process?

545. Will tasks be marked complete only after QA has been successfully completed?

546. Change Management vs. Change Leadership - What's the Difference?

547. What actions will be taken to mitigate the risk?

548. Will there be documented contingency plans for the top 5-10 risks?

549. Will all tasks resulting from issues be entered into the HCISSP Project Plan and tracked through the plan?

550. Is an Issue Management Process documented and filed?

551. Do you anticipate new stakeholders joining the HCISSP Project over time?

552. Is there a Quality Assurance Plan documented and filed?

553. How will you verify the accuracy of the work of the HCISSP Project, and what constitutes acceptance of the deliverables?

554. Any new risks introduced or old risks impacted. Are there issues that could affect the existing requirements for the result, service, or product if the scope changes?

555. If you were to write a list of what should not be included in the scope statement, what are some of the things that you would recommend be described as out-of-scope?

556. Were potential customers involved early in the planning process?

557. Was planning completed before the HCISSP Project was initiated?

558. How often will scope changes be reviewed?

HCISSP: Contract Close-Out

559. A change in knowledge?

560. A change in attitude or behavior?

561. A change in circumstances?

562. What happens to the recipient of services?

563. Why Outsource?

564. What is Capture Management?

565. How does it work?

HCISSP: Activity List

566. How will it be performed?

567. What did not go as well?

568. When will the work be performed?

569. Should you include sub-activities?

570. What is the probability the HCISSP Project can be completed in xx weeks?

571. How much slack is available in the HCISSP Project?

572. Is infrastructure setup part of your HCISSP Project?

573. In what sequence?

574. How detailed should a HCISSP Project get?

575. What will be performed?

576. Where will it be performed?

577. Can you determine the activity that must finish, before this activity can start?

578. What went well?

579. What are the critical bottleneck activities?

580. Who will perform the work?

HCISSP: Schedule Management Plan

581. Are there any activities or deliverables being added or gold-plated that could be dropped or scaled back without falling short of the original requirement?

582. Does the schedule have reasonable float?

583. Are right task and resource calendars used in the IMS?

584. Does the IMS reflect accurate current status and credible start/finish forecasts for all to-go tasks and milestones?

585. What is the estimated time to complete the HCISSP Project if status quo is maintained?

586. Have reserves been created to address risks?

587. Do HCISSP Project managers participating in the HCISSP Project know the HCISSP Projects true status first hand?

588. Why Conduct Schedule Analysis?

589. Is a process defined for baseline approval and control?

590. Why Time Management?

591. Is the critical path valid?

592. Are decisions captured in a decisions log?

593. Are the HCISSP Project team members located locally to the users/stakeholders?

594. Are risk oriented checklists used during risk identification?

595. Have adequate resources been provided by management to ensure HCISSP Project success?

596. Where is the scheduling tool and who has access to it to view it?

597. Were HCISSP Project team members involved in the development of activity & task decomposition?

HCISSP: Probability and Impact Assessment

598. Who are the international/overseas HCISSP Project partners (equipment supplier/supplier/consultant/contractor) for this HCISSP Project?

599. What are the uncertainties associated with the technology selected for the HCISSP Project?

600. Mitigation -how can you avoid the risk?

601. Supply/demand HCISSP Projections and trends; what are the levels of accuracy?

602. Are team members trained in the use of the tools?

603. Do you have a consistent repeatable process that is actually used?

604. When and how will the recent breakthroughs in basic research lead to commercial products?

605. What should be the external organizations responsibility vis-à-vis total stake in the HCISSP Project?

606. What are the risks involved in appointing external agencies to manage the HCISSP Project?

607. Who will be responsible for a slippage?

608. What are the current requirements of the customer?

609. How will the consumption pattern change?

610. How will economic events and trends likely affect the HCISSP Project?

611. How much is the probability of a risk occurring?

612. What are the probabilities of chosen technologies being suitable for local conditions?

613. Is a software HCISSP Project management tool available?

614. What will be the impact or consequence if the risk occurs?

615. Which functions, departments, and activities of the organization are going to be affected?

616. How do risks change during the HCISSP Projects life cycle?

HCISSP: WBS Dictionary

617. Does the accounting system provide a basis for auditing records of direct costs chargeable to the contract?

618. Are current budgets resulting from changes to the authorized work and/or internal replanning, reconcilable to original budgets for specified reporting items?

619. Is the anticipated (firm and potential) business base HCISSP Projected in a rational, consistent manner?

620. Are authorized changes being incorporated in a timely manner?

621. Are estimates of costs at completion utilized in determining contract funding requirements and reporting them?

622. Are current work performance indicators and goals relatable to original goals as modified by contractual changes, replanning, and reprogramming actions?

623. Are direct or indirect cost adjustments being accomplished according to accounting procedures acceptable to us?

624. Does the contractors system identify work accomplishment against the schedule plan?

625. Do the lines of authority for incurring indirect costs correspond to the lines of responsibility for management control of the same components of costs?

626. All CWBS elements specified for external reporting?

627. Are procedures established to prevent changes to the contract budget base other than those authorized by contractual action?

628. Identify and isolate causes of favorable and unfavorable cost and schedule variances?

629. Are retroactive changes to BCWS and BCWP prohibited except for correction of errors or for normal accounting adjustments?

630. Are the responsibilities and authorities of each of the above organizational elements or managers clearly defined?

631. Is cost performance measurement at the point in time most suitable for the category of material involved, but no earlier than the time of actual receipt of material?

632. How Do you Manage Scope?

633. Is each control account assigned to a single organizational element directly responsible for the work and identifiable to a single element of the CWBS?

634. Are HCISSP Projected overhead costs in each

pool and the associated direct costs used as the basis for establishing interim rates for allocating overhead to contracts?

HCISSP: Cost Estimating Worksheet

635. What info is needed?

636. What Can Be Included?

637. How will the results be shared and to whom?

638. Is the HCISSP Project responsive to community need?

639. What will others want?

640. Does the HCISSP Project provide innovative ways for stakeholders to overcome obstacles or deliver better outcomes?

641. Will the HCISSP Project collaborate with the local community and leverage resources?

642. Can a trend be established from historical performance data on the selected measure and are the criteria for using trend analysis or forecasting methods met?

643. What costs are to be estimated?

644. What is the estimated labor cost today based upon this information?

645. What additional HCISSP Project(s) could be initiated as a result of this HCISSP Project?

646. Value Pocket Identification & Quantification What

Are Value Pockets?

647. What happens to any remaining funds not used?

648. Ask: are others positioned to know, are others credible, and will others cooperate?

649. What is the purpose of estimating?

650. Who is best positioned to know and assist in identifying such factors?

651. Identify the timeframe necessary to monitor progress and collect data to determine how the selected measure has changed?

652. Is it feasible to establish a control group arrangement?

HCISSP: Probability and Impact Matrix

653. How realistic is the timing of introduction?

654. Can the risk be avoided by choosing a different alternative?

655. What is HCISSP Project Risk Management?

656. Is the customer willing to establish rapid communication links with the developer?

657. Brain storm – mind maps, what if?

658. Prioritized components/features?

659. Is the number of people on the HCISSP Project team adequate to do the job?

660. What is the best method for analysing the risks for different types of HCISSP Projects?

661. Has something like this been done before?

662. Can you handle the investment risk?

663. What is the probability of the risk occurring?

664. Are the risk data timely and relevant?

665. How are risks and risk management perceived in the HCISSP Project?

666. How solid is the HCISSP Projection of competitive reaction?

667. Are the best people available?

668. Have you ascribed a level of confidence to every critical technical objective?

669. How much is the probability of the risk occurring?

670. What are the current demands of the customer?

HCISSP: Process Improvement Plan

671. Have the supporting tools been developed or acquired?

672. Are there forms and procedures to collect and record the data?

673. Does our process ensure quality?

674. How Do you Manage Quality?

675. Does explicit definition of the measures exist?

676. Where do you focus?

677. What personnel are the champions for the initiative?

678. Why do you want to achieve the goal?

679. Purpose of Goal: The motive is determined by asking, Why do I want to achieve this goal?

680. What Lessons Have you Learned So Far?

681. Are you following the quality standards?

682. Have storage and access mechanisms and procedures been determined?

683. What is quality and how will you ensure it?

684. Are you meeting the quality standards?

685. If a Process Improvement Framework Is Being Used, Which Elements Will Help the Problems and Goals Listed?

686. What Actions Are Needed to Address the Problems and Achieve the Goals?

687. Modeling current processes is great, but will you ever see a return on that investment?

688. What Is the Test-Cycle Concept?

689. Has a process guide to collect the data been developed?

690. To elicit goal statements, do you ask a question such as, What do you want to achieve?

HCISSP: Quality Management Plan

691. Sampling Part of Task?

692. How are data handled when a test is not run per specification?

693. How do senior leaders create and communicate values and performance expectations?

694. Were the right locations/samples tested for the right parameters?

695. How are calibration records kept?

696. How does your organization address regulatory, legal, and ethical compliance?

697. What s the Difference Between a QMP and QAPP?

698. How are records kept in the office?

699. How do you check in-coming sample material?

700. Have all stakeholders been identified?

701. What worked well?

702. Is a component/condition present?

703. Who is Responsible for Approving the QAPP?

704. Who Needs a QMP?

705. Would impacts defined serve as impediments?

706. Have all involved stakeholders and work groups committed to the HCISSP Project?

707. What is Quality Planning ?

HCISSP: Stakeholder Register

708. What & Why?

709. What opportunities exist to provide communications?

710. Is Your Organization Ready for Change?

711. How much influence do they have on the HCISSP Project?

712. How will Reports Be Created?

713. How should employers make their voices heard?

714. What are the major HCISSP Project milestones requiring communications or providing communications opportunities?

715. Who is Managing Stakeholder Engagement?

716. What is the power of the stakeholder?

717. How Big is the Gap?

718. Who wants to talk about Security?

HCISSP: Team Operating Agreement

719. Do you ensure that all participants know how to use the required technology?

720. What are the current caseload numbers in the unit?

721. Are team roles clearly defined and accepted?

722. Did you recap the meeting purpose, time, and expectations?

723. Did you draft the meeting agenda?

724. Must your members collaborate successfully to complete HCISSP Projects?

725. Do you upload presentation materials in advance and test the technology?

726. What types of accommodations will be formulated and put in place for sustaining the team?

727. Do you post meeting notes and the recording (if used) and notify participants?

728. What is your unique contribution to the organization?

729. How will you resolve conflict efficiently and respectfully?

730. Are leadership responsibilities shared among

team members (versus a single leader)?

731. Reimbursements: How will the team members be reimbursed for expenses and time commitments?

732. What is Culture?

733. What administrative supports will be put in place to support the team and the teams supervisor?

734. Conflict Resolution: How will disputes and other conflicts be mediated or resolved?

735. What individual strengths does each team member bring to the group?

736. What is the anticipated procedure (recruitment, solicitation of volunteers, or assignment) for selecting team members?

737. What are the safety issues/risks that need to be addressed and/or that the team needs to discuss?

738. What are the boundaries (organizational or geographic) within which you operate?

HCISSP: Contractor Status Report

739. Who can list a HCISSP Project as company experience, the company or a previous employee of the company?

740. How is Risk Transferred?

741. What was the overall budget or estimated cost?

742. What are the minimum and optimal bandwidth requirements for the proposed soluiton?

743. What was the actual budget or estimated cost for your companys services?

744. What was the final actual cost?

745. What was the budget or estimated cost for your companys services?

HCISSP: Scope Management Plan

746. Is mitigation authorized or recommended?

747. Which statement about customer expectations is not true?

748. Have the procedures for identifying variances from estimates & adjusting the detailed work program been followed?

749. Is there a HCISSP Project organization chart showing the reporting relationships and responsibilities for each position?

750. Has the selected plan been formulated using cost effectiveness and incremental analysis techniques?

751. Have activity relationships and interdependencies within tasks been adequately identified?

752. Have the key functions and capabilities been defined and assigned to each release or iteration?

753. Are staffing resource estimates sufficiently detailed and documented for use in planning and tracking the HCISSP Project?

754. Is the organization structure for both tracking & controlling the budget well defined and assigned to a specific individual?

755. Has a provision been made to reassess HCISSP

Project risks at various HCISSP Project stages?

756. Are software metrics formally captured, analyzed and used as a basis for other HCISSP Project estimates?

757. Does the Resource Management Plan include a personnel development plan?

758. Does the implementation plan have an appropriate division of responsibilities?

759. What do you need to do to accomplish the goal or goals?

760. What is the relative power of the HCISSP Project manager?

761. Are changes in deliverable commitments agreed to by all affected groups & individuals?

HCISSP: Cost Baseline

762. Vac -variance at completion, how much over/under budget do you expect to be?

763. Have the lessons learned been filed with the HCISSP Project Management Office?

764. HCISSP Project Goals -should others be reconsidered?

765. How likely is it to go wrong?

766. Has the HCISSP Project documentation been archived or otherwise disposed as described in the HCISSP Project communication plan?

767. What deliverables come first?

768. How long are you willing to wait before you find out were late?

769. What s the reality?

770. What is Cost and HCISSP Project Cost Management?

771. Has the appropriate access to relevant data and analysis capability been granted?

772. What is the most important thing to do next to make your HCISSP Project successful?

773. Is request in line with priorities?

774. Has training and knowledge transfer of the operations organization been completed?

775. What does it mean to say a task is 75% complete after 3 months?

776. Has the HCISSP Project (or HCISSP Project phase) been evaluated against each objective established in the product description and Integrated HCISSP Project Plan?

777. What is it ?

778. Has the HCISSP Projected annual cost to operate and maintain the product(s) or service(s) been approved and funded?

779. Verify business objectives. Are others appropriate, and well-articulated?

780. What is the consequence?

HCISSP: Earned Value Status

781. How does this compare with other HCISSP Projects?

782. Earned Value can be used in almost any HCISSP Project situation and in almost any HCISSP Project environment. It may be used on large HCISSP Projects, medium sized HCISSP Projects, tiny HCISSP Projects (in cut-down form), complex and simple HCISSP Projects and in any market sector. Some people, of course, know all about earned value, they have used it for years - but perhaps not as effectively as they could have?

783. Are you hitting our HCISSP Projects targets?

784. If earned value management (EVM) is so good in determining the true status of a HCISSP Project and HCISSP Project its completion, why is it that hardly any one uses it in information systems related HCISSP Projects?

HCISSP: Responsibility Assignment Matrix

785. Are the overhead pools formally and adequately identified?

786. Is work properly classified as measured effort, LOE, or apportioned effort and appropriately separated?

787. Who is going to do that work?

788. Are detailed work packages planned as far in advance as practicable?

789. What is the number one predictor of a group s productivity?

790. Is accountability placed at the lowest-possible level within the HCISSP Project so that decisions can be made at that level?

791. Evaluate the impact of schedule changes, work around, etc?

792. Detailed schedules which support control account and work package start and completion dates/events?

793. What is the purpose of assigning and documenting responsibility?

794. Are the WBS and organizational levels for

application of the HCISSP Projected overhead costs identified?

795. What are the constraints?

796. Are the actual costs used for variance analysis reconcilable with data from the accounting system?

797. Performance to date and material commitment?

798. Changes in the direct base to which overhead costs are allocated?

799. Are control accounts opened and closed based on the start and completion of work contained therein?

800. Do managers and team members provide helpful suggestions during review meetings?

801. Too many Rs: With too many people labeled as doing the work, are there too many hands involved?

802. Is every Signing-off responsibility and every Communicating responsibility critically necessary?

HCISSP: Change Request

803. What must be taken into consideration when introducing change control programs?

804. How are changes requested (forms, method of communication)?

805. Change Request Coordination ?

806. How is the change documented (format, content, storage)?

807. What is the function of the change control committee?

808. What should be regulated in a change control operating instruction?

809. How many times must the change be modified or presented to the change control board before it is approved?

810. When to Submit a Change Request?

811. Are change requests logged and managed?

812. How is quality being addressed on the HCISSP Project?

813. Describe how modifications, enhancements, defects and/or deficiencies shall be notified (e.g. Problem Reports, Change Requests etc) and managed. Detail warranty and/or maintenance

periods?

814. What type of changes does change control take into account?

815. Who can suggest changes?

816. Has a formal technical review been conducted to assess technical correctness?

817. Who has responsibility for approving and ranking changes?

818. Is it feasible to use requirements attributes as predictors of reliability?

819. What needs to be communicated?

820. What is the change request log?

821. What is the purpose of change control?

822. Should staff call into the helpdesk or go to the website?

HCISSP: Change Log

823. Do the described changes impact on the integrity or security of the system?

824. Is the submitted change a new change or a modification of a previously approved change?

825. Is the change backward compatible without limitations?

826. Is the change request within HCISSP Project scope?

827. Does the suggested change request represent a desired enhancement to the products functionality?

828. How does this relate to the standards developed for specific business processes?

829. Will the HCISSP Project fail if the change request is not executed?

830. How does this change affect the timeline of the schedule?

831. How does this change affect scope?

832. When was the request submitted?

833. Where Do Changes Come From?

834. Does the suggested change request seem to represent a necessary enhancement to the product?

835. Is the requested change request a result of changes in other HCISSP Project(s)?

836. Who initiated the change request?

837. Is the change request open, closed or pending?

838. Is this a mandatory replacement?

839. Should a more thorough impact analysis be conducted?

840. When was the request approved?

HCISSP: Source Selection Criteria

841. Do you have a plan to document consensus results including disposition of any disagreement by individual evaluators?

842. What Should Be Discussed?

843. Who is Entitled to a Debriefing?

844. Which contract type places the most risk on the seller?

845. Is the offeror pricing what is technically proposed?

846. Are evaluators ready to begin this task?

847. What documentation should be used to support the selection decision?

848. When and what information can be discussed with offerors regarding past performance?

849. How long will it take for the purchase cost to be the same as the lease cost?

850. Is a cost realism analysis used?

851. How do you facilitate evaluation against published criteria?

852. How are oral presentations documented?

853. What are the steps in performing a cost/tech tradeoff?

854. What management structure does the organization consider as optimal for performing the contract?

855. What is the effect of the debriefing schedule on potential protests?

856. What benefits are accrued from issuing a DRFP in advance of issuing a final RFP?

857. What should be the contracting officers strategy?

858. What are the most critical evaluation criteria that prove to be tiebreakers in the evaluation of proposals?

859. Is a letter of commitment from each proposed team member and key subcontractor included?

860. What Can Not Be Disclosed?

HCISSP: HCISSP Project Management Plan

861. What are the assumptions?

862. What is risk management?

863. Are the proposed HCISSP Project purposes different than a previously authorized HCISSP Project?

864. Are the existing and future without-plan conditions reasonable and appropriate?

865. Who Manages Integration?

866. What are the assigned resources?

867. Why Do you Manage Integration?

868. How do you organize the costs in the HCISSP Project management plan?

869. What data/reports/tools/etc. do your PMs need?

870. Why Change?

871. Does the selected plan protect privacy?

872. What are the training needs?

873. Is the appropriate plan selected based on the organizations objectives and evaluation criteria expressed in Principles and Guidelines policies?

874. Will you add a schedule and diagram?

875. Was the peer (technical) review of the cost estimates duly coordinated with the cost estimate center of expertise and addressed in the review documentation and certification?

HCISSP: HCISSP Project Schedule

876. Are all remaining durations correct?

877. Eliminate unnecessary activities. Are there activities that came from a template or previous HCISSP Project that are not applicable on this phase of this HCISSP Project?

878. Are procedures defined by which the HCISSP Project schedule may be changed?

879. Why or why not?

880. Understand the constraints used in preparing the schedule. Are activities connected because logic dictates the order in which others occur?

881. A master HCISSP Project schedule?

882. Your HCISSP Project management plan results in a HCISSP Project schedule that is too long. If the HCISSP Project network diagram cannot change but you have extra personnel resources, what is the BEST thing to do?

883. Are quality inspections and review activities listed in the HCISSP Project schedule(s)?

884. It allows the HCISSP Project to be delivered on schedule. How Do you Use Schedules?

885. If there are any qualifying green components to this HCISSP Project, what portion of the total HCISSP

Project cost is green?

886. Should you have a test for each code module?

887. Are there activities that came from a template or previous HCISSP Project that are not applicable on this phase of this HCISSP Project?

888. What is HCISSP Project Management?

889. What is the most mis-scheduled part of process?

890. What is the purpose of a HCISSP Project schedule?

891. How effectively were issues able to be resolved without impacting the HCISSP Project Schedule or Budget?

892. Change Management Required?

HCISSP: HCISSP Project Performance Report

893. What is the PRS?

894. Next Steps?

895. How is the data used?

896. How can HCISSP Project Sustainability be Maintained?

897. What s in it for you?

HCISSP: Resource Breakdown Structure

898. How can this help you with team building?

899. Changes Based on Input from Stakeholders?

900. What is each stakeholders desired outcome for the HCISSP Project?

901. How should the information be delivered?

902. Any Changes from Stakeholders?

903. What is the number one predictor of a groups productivity?

904. What is the primary purpose of the human resource plan?

905. What s the difference between % Complete and % work?

906. Who is allowed to perform which functions?

907. When do they need the information?

908. Which resources should be in the resource pool?

909. Is Predictive Resource Analysis being done?

910. Who is allowed to see what data about which resources?

911. Which resource planning tool provides information on resource responsibility and accountability?

912. Who needs what information?

HCISSP: HCISSP Project or Phase Close-Out

913. Was the schedule met?

914. What could have been improved?

915. Were cost budgets met?

916. What is a Risk?

917. What were the desired outcomes?

918. Planned Completion Date?

919. What is this stakeholder expecting?

920. What are they?

921. What is a Risk Management Process?

922. What was learned?

923. Planned Remaining Costs ()?

924. What were the actual outcomes?

925. Complete Yes or No?

HCISSP: Requirements Traceability Matrix

926. What is the WBS?

927. How small is small enough?

928. What percentage of HCISSP Projects are producing traceability matrices between requirements and other work products?

929. How will it affect the stakeholders personally in their career?

930. What are the chronologies, contingencies, consequences, criteria?

931. Why Do you Manage Scope?

932. Will you use a Requirements Traceability Matrix?

933. Is there a requirements traceability process in place?

934. Do we have a clear understanding of all subcontracts in place?

935. Why use a WBS?

936. Describe the process for approving requirements so they can be added to the traceability matrix and HCISSP Project work can be performed. Will the HCISSP Project requirements become approved in

writing?

HCISSP: Variance Analysis

937. Budgeted cost for work performed?

938. Did a new competitor enter the market?

939. How does your company measure performance?

940. Did an existing competitor change their strategy?

941. What should management do?

942. Favorable or Unfavorable Variance?

943. The anticipated business volume?

944. Historical experience?

945. Is there a logical explanation for any variance?

946. Why are standard cost systems used?

947. Contract line items and end items?

948. Why do variances exist?

HCISSP: Risk Audit

949. Are some people working on multiple HCISSP Projects?

950. Risks with HCISSP Projects or new initiatives?

951. Are end-users enthusiastically committed to the HCISSP Project and the system/product to be built?

952. Are HCISSP Project requirements stable?

HCISSP: Initiating Process Group

953. Who is performing the work of the HCISSP Project?

954. How well did the chosen processes produce the expected results?

955. During which stage of Risk planning are risks prioritized based on probability and impact?

956. During which stage of Risk planning are modeling techniques used to determine overall effects of risks on HCISSP Project objectives for high probability, high impact risks?

957. Which Six Sigma DMAIC phase focuses on why and how defects and errors occur?

958. What areas were overlooked on this HCISSP Project?

959. What is the NEXT thing to do?

960. The process to Manage Stakeholders is part of which process group?

961. Am I just doing busywork to pass the time?

962. How do you help others satisfy their needs?

963. Were sponsors and decision makers available when needed outside regularly scheduled meetings?

964. Who are the HCISSP Project stakeholders?

965. Are you properly tracking the progress of the HCISSP Project and communicating the status to stakeholders?

966. If action is called for, what form should it take?

HCISSP: Procurement Management Plan

967. What types of contracts will be used?

968. Has the scope management document been updated and distributed to help prevent scope creep?

969. Is PERT / Critical Path or equivalent methodology being used?

970. Are updated HCISSP Project time & resource estimates reasonable based on the current HCISSP Project stage?

971. Specific - Is the objective clear in terms of what, how, when, and where the situation will be changed?

972. What communication items need improvement?

973. Are there checklists created to determine if all quality processes are followed?

974. Are target dates established for each milestone deliverable?

975. Is the HCISSP Project Sponsor clearly communicating the Business Case or rationale for why this HCISSP Project is needed?

976. Is there a procurement management plan in place?

977. Staffing Requirements?

978. Does the HCISSP Project have a formal HCISSP Project Charter?

979. Are assumptions being identified, recorded, analyzed, qualified and closed?

HCISSP: Decision Log

980. What is the average size of your matters in an applicable measurement?

981. Decision-making process; how will the team make decisions?

982. Do strategies and tactics aimed at less than full control reduce the costs of management or simply shift the cost burden?

983. Adversarial Environment. Is your opponent open to a non-traditional workflow, or will it likely challenge anything you do?

984. Meeting purpose; why does this team meet?

985. Who will be given a copy of this document and where will it be kept?

986. How does an increasing emphasis on cost containment influence the strategies and tactics used?

987. What makes you different or better than others companies selling the same thing?

988. Does anything need to be adjusted?

989. How effective is maintaining the log at facilitating organizational learning?

990. Which variables make a critical difference?

991. At what point in time does loss become unacceptable?

992. How do you know when you are achieving it?

993. Is everything working as expected?

994. So, what is the line where eDiscovery ends and document review begins?

995. It becomes critical to track and periodically revisit both operational effectiveness; Are you noticing all that you need to, and are you interpreting what you see effectively?

996. What was the rationale for the decision?

997. What alternatives/risks were considered?

998. How consolidated and comprehensive a story can we tell by capturing currently available incident data in a central location and through a log of key decisions during an incident?

999. How do you define success?

HCISSP: Duration Estimating Worksheet

1000. When does the organization expect to be able to complete it?

1001. Done before proceeding with this activity or what can be done concurrently?

1002. What s an Average HCISSP Project?

1003. When, then?

1004. How can the HCISSP Project be displayed graphically to better visualize the activities?

1005. Why Estimate Costs?

1006. What work will be included in the HCISSP Project?

1007. What questions do you have?

1008. When do the individual activities need to start and finish?

1009. Small or Large HCISSP Project?

1010. Does the HCISSP Project provide innovative ways for Veterans to overcome obstacles or deliver better outcomes?

1011. Is this operation cost effective?

1012. What's Next?

1013. Is a Construction detail attached (to aid in explanation)?

1014. How should ongoing costs be monitored to try to keep the HCISSP Project within budget?

HCISSP: Activity Attributes

1015. Which method produces the more accurate cost assignment?

1016. How many resources do you need to complete the work scope within a limit of X number of days?

1017. Activity: Whats In the Bag?

1018. Resource is assigned to?

1019. Has management defined a definite timeframe for the turnaround or HCISSP Project window?

1020. Does the organization of the data change its meaning?

1021. Whats Missing?

1022. How many days do you need to complete the work scope with a limit of X number of resources?

1023. How difficult will it be to complete specific activities on this HCISSP Project?

1024. What is the organization s history in doing similar activities?

1025. How Much Activity Detail Is Required?

1026. Is there a trend during the year?

1027. Why?

1028. Activity: Fair or Not Fair?

1029. What activity do you think you should spend the most time on?

1030. Can more resources be added?

1031. Can you re-assign any activities to another resource to resolve an over-allocation?

1032. Have constraints been applied to the start and finish milestones for the phases?

HCISSP: HCISSP Project Charter

1033. Market – Identify products market, including whether it is outside of the objective: What is the purpose of the program or HCISSP Project?

1034. Strategic Fit: What is the Strategic Initiative Identifier for this HCISSP Project?

1035. What are the known stakeholder requirements?

1036. Why the Improvements?

1037. Dependent HCISSP Projects: What HCISSP Projects must be underway or completed before this HCISSP Project can be successful?

1038. Environmental Stewardship and Sustainability Considerations: What is the process that will be used to ensure compliance with the Environmental Stewardship Policy?

1039. Is it an improvement over existing products?

1040. Major High-Level Milestone Targets: What events measure progress?

1041. Whose input and support will this HCISSP Project require?

1042. Must Have?

1043. Success Determination Factors: How will the success of the HCISSP Project be determined from the customers perspective?

1044. Who will take notes, document decisions?

1045. Run it as as a startup?

1046. Does the HCISSP Project need to consider any special capacity or capability issues?

1047. Customer Benefits: What customer requirements does this HCISSP Project address?

1048. What is the justification?

1049. When is a charter needed?

1050. Why have you chosen the aim you have set forth?

HCISSP: Change Management Plan

1051. Will the readiness criteria be met prior to the training roll out?

1052. Would you need to tailor a special message for each segment of the audience?

1053. Will the culture embrace or reject this change?

1054. What will be the preferred method of delivery?

1055. Who is the target audience of the piece of information?

1056. What communication network would you use – informal or formal?

1057. What is the reason for the communication?

1058. What are you trying to achieve as a result of communication?

1059. Have the approved procedures and policies been published?

1060. When to start change management?

1061. What new roles are needed?

1062. Readiness -What is a successful end state?

1063. Has this been negotiated with the customer and sponsor?

1064. What risks may occur upfront?

1065. Who will be the change levers?

1066. Clearly articulate the overall business benefits of the HCISSP Project -why are you doing this now?

1067. What risks may occur upfront, during implementation and after implementation?

1068. Have the systems been configured and tested?

1069. What is the most positive interpretation it can receive?

1070. What are the current methods of sharing information and do there need to be new ones developed?

HCISSP: Team Member Performance Assessment

1071. Why were these selected?

1072. What are top priorities?

1073. What makes them effective?

1074. Who they are?

1075. How will they be formed?

1076. Who is responsible?

1077. Goals met?

1078. What is collaboration?

1079. Who should attend?

1080. Why do performance reviews?

1081. Did training work?

HCISSP: Issue Log

1082. What is the impact on the risks?

1083. Who needs to know and how much?

1084. Are they needed?

1085. Do you feel a register helps?

1086. Why Do you Manage Communications?

1087. What is the status of the issue?

1088. What is a change?

1089. What is a Stakeholder?

1090. Who is the issue assigned to?

1091. What would have to change?

1092. What approaches do you use?

HCISSP: Monitoring and Controlling Process Group

1093. Where is the Risk in the HCISSP Project?

1094. What is the expected monetary value of the HCISSP Project?

1095. What do they need to know about the HCISSP Project?

1096. How many potential communications channels exist on the HCISSP Project?

1097. What is the timeline for the HCISSP Project?

1098. Did the HCISSP Project team have the right skills?

1099. How is Agile HCISSP Project Management Done?

1100. What were things that you did very well and want to do the same again on the next HCISSP Project?

1101. A HCISSP Project management team of two has 8 key stakeholders to work with. How many potential communications channels exist on the HCISSP Project?

Index

abilities 111
ability 27, 64, 143
abnormal   108
acceptable   40, 59, 144, 170
acceptance 4, 21, 99, 111, 145, 150, 162
accepted   90, 182
access 2, 8-9, 37, 45, 143, 167, 177, 187
accomplish   7, 39, 55, 89, 133, 144, 186
according   29, 33, 145, 161, 170
account   10, 31, 171, 190, 193
accounted   42
accounting   170-171, 191
accounts   191
accrued   197
accuracy   45, 111, 162, 168
accurate   9, 79, 123, 166, 218
Achievable   95, 144
achieve   7, 48, 57, 95, 108, 112, 115, 128, 145, 177-178, 222
achieved   16, 58, 82, 145, 148
achieving   103, 146, 215
acquire   109
acquired   118, 177
across 37, 74
action 39, 74-75, 122, 171, 211
actionable   98, 146
actions 21, 69, 77, 104, 133, 143, 155, 161, 170, 178
active 141
activities   20, 55, 72, 104, 117, 125, 129-130, 146-147, 155-156, 164, 166, 169, 200-201, 216, 218-219
activity 3-4, 6, 24, 30, 103, 117-118, 125, 130-131, 133, 155-156, 159-160, 164, 167, 185, 216, 218-219
actual 30, 120, 171, 184, 191, 205
actually   27, 56, 67, 77, 107, 144, 168
addition   8, 97, 143
additional   25, 46-47, 50-51, 123, 133, 173
additions   72
address   17, 62, 166, 178-179, 221
addressed   136, 159, 183, 192, 199
addressing   27, 90
adequate   167, 175

adequately   25, 45, 185, 190
adhering   146
adjusted   214
adjusting   185
adopters   140
advance   122, 182, 190, 197
advantage   48, 94
advantages   98-99, 137
advise 8
affect 47, 50-51, 92, 103-104, 137, 162, 169, 194, 206
affected   105, 169, 186
affecting   12, 19, 49
affects 125
afford   121
against 31, 66, 170, 188, 196
agencies   91, 168
agenda   182
Aggregate   37
Agility   115
agreed   39, 44, 149, 186
Agreement   5, 92, 111, 182
agreements   123
agrees 100
aiming 95, 112
alerting   149
alerts   74
aligned   17, 83, 115
alignment   43
alleged   1
allocate   90
allocated   95, 191
allocating   172
allowed   85-86, 203
allows 9, 130, 200
almost 189
already   88, 110
always 9
Amazon   10
ambitious   127
America   27
amount   142, 154
amplify 51, 78
analysed   129

analysing 175
analysis 3, 5, 11, 34, 36-38, 40-43, 46-47, 49-50, 53, 60-63, 106-107, 111, 126, 137, 143, 150, 166, 173, 185, 187, 191, 195-196, 203, 208
analyze 2, 36-38, 44-47, 50, 57
analyzed 36, 38, 41, 44-45, 62, 74, 186, 213
annual 188
another 10, 96, 114, 219
answer 11-12, 16, 23, 34, 46, 54, 66, 76
answered 22, 33, 45, 53, 64, 75, 101
answering 11
Answers 145
anticipate 162
anyone 31, 83, 94, 137
anything 107, 152, 159, 214
appear 1
applicable 12, 146, 200-201, 214
applied 71, 219
appointed 31-32
appointing 168
approach 98, 109, 116, 155
approaches 60, 225
approval 29, 87, 166
approved 142, 188, 192, 194-195, 206, 222
approving 179, 193, 206
Architects 7
archived 187
around 85, 190
arriving 123
articulate 223
ascribed 176
asking 1, 7, 177
aspect 140
assess 18, 62, 126, 130, 193
assessing 57, 70
Assessment 3-4, 6, 8-9, 20, 120, 127, 149, 168, 224
assets 153
assign 19
assigned 31, 113, 134, 171, 185, 198, 218, 225
assigning 190
assignment 5, 183, 190, 218
assist 59, 152, 174
assistant 7

associated   157, 168, 172
Assumption   3, 141
Assurance   105-106, 135, 143, 162
assure 45, 60
attached   217
attainable   29, 144
attempted   31
attempting   68
attend 224
attendance   32
attendant   61
attended   32
attending   151
attention   12, 79, 151
attitude   163
attitudes   110
attracted   112
Attributes   6, 84, 193, 218
audience   222
audited   111
auditing   17, 71, 170
audits 119
auspices   8
author 1
authority   132, 144, 147, 149, 171
authorized   125, 170-171, 185, 198
available   18, 21, 25, 33, 41, 47, 51, 80, 118, 130, 151, 164, 169, 176, 210, 215
Average   12, 22, 33, 45, 53, 64, 75, 101, 214, 216
avoided   175
avoiding   152
awareness   117
background   10
backup   127
backward   194
balance   37
balancing   116
bandwidth   184
barriers 44, 139
Baseline   5, 43, 161, 166, 187
baselined   35, 105
baselines   24, 33
Beauty 93

because 37, 45, 200
become 81, 89, 99, 206, 215
becomes 215
before 9, 31, 70, 111, 130-131, 151, 162, 164, 175, 187, 192, 216, 220
beginning 2, 15, 22, 33, 45, 53, 65, 75, 101
begins 215
behavior 26, 163
behaviors 137
belief 11, 16, 23, 34, 46, 54, 66, 76, 90
believable 95
believe 90, 100
benchmark 108
benefit 1, 18, 21, 62, 68, 111, 121, 137
benefits 20, 50-51, 76, 82, 85, 94, 96, 116, 131-132, 135, 142, 157, 197, 221, 223
better 7, 32, 36, 44, 123, 134, 136-137, 173, 214, 216
between 35, 37, 49, 106, 139, 141-142, 179, 203, 206
biggest 42, 58, 107, 116, 154
blinding 53
Blokdyk 8
bottleneck 164
bought 10
bounce 49, 52
boundaries 32, 183
bounds 32
Breakdown 3, 5, 64, 113, 203
briefed 31
brings 27
broken 47
brought 86
budget 64, 74, 80, 105, 120, 132, 145, 153, 171, 184-185, 187, 201, 217
Budgeted 208
budgets 100, 144, 170, 205
building 21, 74, 203
burden 214
business 1, 7, 10, 16-17, 21, 23-26, 28, 31, 42-43, 51-52, 57, 74-75, 77-79, 82-83, 87-88, 95, 99, 107, 112, 115, 136, 141, 150, 156-158, 170, 188, 194, 208, 212, 223
busywork 210
button 10
Buy-in 81

Calculate 118
calculated 132
calendars 166
called 211
cannot 125, 200
capability 18, 44, 187, 221
capable 7, 26
capacities 85
capacity 18, 21, 135, 221
capital 76
Capture 74, 163
captured 35, 76, 111, 123, 166, 186
capturing 215
career 144, 206
careers 100
cascaded 83
cascading 38
caseload 182
category 27, 32, 171
caused 1
causes 34, 46, 48, 50, 53, 69, 171
causing 19
center 199
central 215
certain 56, 125
chaired 8
challenge 7, 37, 214
challenged 93, 120
challenges 87, 99, 112
Champagne 8
champion 28
champions 177
chance 128
change 5-6, 16, 24, 51-52, 58, 62, 64, 67, 76, 91, 93, 111, 113, 115-116, 123, 149, 156, 161, 163, 169, 181, 192-195, 198, 200-201, 208, 218, 222-223, 225
changed 24, 84, 100, 174, 200, 212
changes 20, 45, 58-59, 61, 70, 72, 82, 95, 99, 134, 142, 144, 149, 162, 170-171, 186, 190-195, 203
changing 85
channels 226
chargeable 170
charter 6, 24-25, 104, 123, 213, 220-221

charters 31
charts 38-39, 48
cheaper 36, 44
checked 69, 74, 157
checklist 8, 85
checklists 167, 212
choice 27, 32, 81
choose 11, 104
choosing 175
chosen 124, 153, 169, 210, 221
circumvent 17
claimed 1
classified 190
cleaning 27
clearly 11, 16, 23, 27-29, 34, 46, 54, 66, 76, 143, 157, 161, 171, 182, 212, 223
client 8, 10, 39, 86, 126, 145
clients 32
closed 67, 124, 191, 195, 213
closely 10
Close-Out 4-5, 155, 163, 205
closest 77
Closing 4, 51, 153
Coaches 25, 31
coding 141
coherent 112
colleague 88
colleagues 90
collect 45, 133, 174, 177-178
collected 29, 32, 40, 43, 47, 51, 62, 125
collection 34-37, 42, 47
college 59
coming 47
command 72
commercial 168
commitment 97, 123, 191, 197
committed 25, 77, 151, 180, 209
committee 141, 192
common 155
community 122, 128, 149-150, 173
companies 1, 8, 214
company 7, 36, 44, 48, 78-79, 83, 88, 96, 99, 111, 117, 184, 208

companys	117, 184
compare	53, 59, 120-121, 189
compared	83, 105, 132
Comparing	60
comparison	11
compatible	194
compelling	25
competitor	208
complain	107
complete	1, 8, 11, 20, 25, 107, 123, 126, 130, 145, 151, 161, 166, 182, 188, 203, 205, 216, 218
completed	12, 24, 26, 28, 126, 130-131, 161-162, 164, 188, 220
completely	87
completing	89, 114
completion	24, 29, 59, 131, 153, 170, 187, 189-191, 205
complex	7, 40, 99, 189
complexity	36
compliance	47, 179, 220
complied	133
complies	132
comply	132
component	179
components	38-39, 141, 152, 171, 175, 200
comprise	104
compute	12
computing	87
concept	55, 117, 178
Concern	144
concerns	20, 44, 77, 139
concise	149
condition	69, 179
conditions	69, 98, 133, 169, 198
Conduct	166
conducted	63, 119, 124, 193, 195
conducting	51
confidence	176
confident	131
configured	223
confirm	11
Conflict	182-183
conflicts	86, 157, 183
conform	142

conjure	158
connected	200
connecting	98
consensus	196
consider	17, 19, 75, 116, 197, 221
considered	17-18, 35, 132, 215
considers	48
consistent	36, 70, 104, 146-147, 155, 168, 170
Constraint	3, 141
consultant	7, 168
consulted	80
consulting	43
consumers	100
Contact	7
contacts	86
contain	16, 67
contained	1, 191
contains	8
content	32, 146, 192
contents	1-2, 8
continual	10, 67, 73
Continuity	117
continuum	94
contract	4, 105, 109, 133, 163, 170-171, 196-197, 208
contracted	156
Contractor	5, 149, 168, 184
contracts	29, 124, 135, 172, 212
control	2, 64, 66-68, 70-73, 105, 166, 171, 174, 190-193, 214
controlled	48, 122
controls	16, 47-48, 56, 64, 68-72, 74, 128, 132
convenient	37, 45
convention	100
conversion	141
convey	1
cooperate	174
Copyright	1
correct	34, 66, 200
correction	171
corrective	69, 121
correspond	8, 10, 171
cosmetic	141
costing	37, 155
counting	98

counts 98
course 24, 189
covering 69, 143
coworker 86
crashing 131
craziest 87
create 10, 17, 39, 78, 81, 98, 179
created 50-51, 84, 104, 122, 128, 166, 181, 212
creating 7, 42
creation 116, 152
creativity 56
credible 166, 174
crisis 22
criteria 2, 5, 8, 10, 21, 27, 29-30, 32, 59, 70, 77, 93, 96, 102, 124, 126, 173, 196-198, 206, 222
CRITERION 2, 16, 23, 34, 46, 54, 66, 76
critical 30, 32, 51, 72, 75, 80, 84, 125, 141, 153, 164, 166, 176, 197, 212, 214-215
critically 191
criticism 50
crucial 51, 135
crystal 12
cultural 56
culture 23, 49, 144, 183, 222
current 28, 34-35, 49-50, 52-53, 74, 84, 86, 89-90, 111, 115, 121-122, 141-143, 153, 166, 169-170, 176, 178, 182, 212, 223
currently 29, 69, 215
custom 19
customer 10, 21, 27, 29, 32-33, 45, 66, 74-75, 80, 82, 84-85, 88, 93, 109, 133, 151, 158, 169, 175-176, 185, 221-222
customers 1, 17, 24, 32-33, 37, 40, 45, 50, 53, 76, 81, 83, 91-94, 98, 118, 129, 134, 142, 162, 221
cut-down 189
damage 1
Dashboard 8
dashboards 72
database 125
day-to-day 73, 98
deadlines 18, 97, 118
debriefing 196-197
deceitful 86
decide 61, 135
deciding 80

decision 6, 52, 56, 59, 62, 196, 210, 214-215
decisions 59, 64, 71, 74, 125, 133-135, 155, 166, 190, 214-215, 221
dedicated 7
deeper 12
deepest 8
defect 44, 107
defects 42, 107, 192, 210
define 2, 23, 25, 27-28, 44, 49, 113, 150, 215
defined 11-12, 16-17, 23-24, 26-30, 32-34, 42, 46, 48, 54, 66, 76, 107, 113, 119, 124, 126, 141, 143, 153, 161, 166, 171, 180, 182, 185, 200, 218
defines 19, 23, 27
Defining 7
definite 67, 218
definition 177
degree 59, 127
delayed 118
Delaying 127
delegated 26
deletions 72
deliver 17, 30, 82, 97, 147, 156, 173, 216
delivered 40, 96, 133, 154, 200, 203
delivering 121
delivery 20, 86, 98, 131, 222
demand 96, 168
demands 111, 176
department 7, 78, 109
depend 110
dependent 86, 138, 220
depends 79
depict 130
deploy 92, 146
deployed 43, 68, 150
deploying 42
derive 70
Describe 21, 63, 117, 149, 192, 206
described 1, 157, 162, 187, 194
describes 125
describing 24, 112
deserving 109
design 1, 8, 10, 27, 61-63, 72, 141
designed 7, 10, 46, 55, 59, 61

designing 7
desired 25, 64, 194, 203, 205
detail 41, 60, 113, 192, 217-218
detailed 46, 51, 164, 185, 190
details 119
detect 69
determine 10-11, 44, 77, 92, 97, 103, 111, 164, 174, 210, 212
determined 48, 92, 177, 220
determines 156
detracting 78
develop 54, 56, 59, 113, 116, 121
developed 8, 10, 25-26, 30-31, 41, 59, 61, 69, 106, 117, 142, 149, 177-178, 194, 223
developer 175
developing 46, 55, 104, 123
diagram 3, 48, 130, 199-200
dictates 200
Dictionary 4, 170
difference 161, 179, 203, 214
different 7, 27, 31, 33, 48, 63, 92, 103, 111, 141-142, 144, 175, 198, 214
difficult 117, 218
dilemma 80
direct 155, 170, 172, 191
direction 24, 36, 44, 83, 115
directions 128
directly 1, 50, 53, 137, 171
Directory 3, 133
Disagree 11, 16, 23, 34, 46, 54, 66, 76
discarded 77
Disclosed 197
discover 149
discovered 57
discuss 183
discussed 196
discussion 37
display 38, 117
displayed 32, 34, 36, 39, 50, 216
disposed 187
disputes 183
disqualify 77
disruptive 52
distribute 133

divergent 104
Divided 22, 26, 33, 45, 53, 64, 75, 101
division 186
document 10, 30, 133, 149, 196, 212, 214-215, 221
documented 32, 41, 67-68, 70, 74, 112, 124, 141, 143, 145, 153, 157, 161-162, 185, 192, 196
documents 7, 142
domain 45
domains 100
dormant 86
driving 90, 94
dropped 166
Duration 3, 6, 103, 113, 125, 129-130, 216
durations 30, 200
during 24, 63, 94, 106-107, 111, 119, 129, 142, 159, 167, 169, 191, 210, 215, 218, 223
dynamics 31
earlier 85, 171
earliest 150
earned 5, 126, 189
easily 125
economic 128, 169
economical 97
economy 64
eDiscovery 215
edition 8
editorial 1
education 18, 69
effect 45, 146, 197
effective 20, 87, 90-91, 100, 119, 146-148, 214, 216, 224
effects 39, 103, 117, 121, 210
efficiency 49, 73
efficient 110, 119
effort 38, 58, 83, 124, 142, 190
efforts 31
electronic 1
element 171
elements 10-11, 67, 92, 112, 134-135, 171, 178
elephant 145
elicit 178
Eliminate 200
embarking 25
embrace 222

emerging 18, 74
emphasis 214
employee 61, 83, 184
employees 52, 78, 89, 92, 96, 98
employers 146, 181
empower 7
enable 52, 74
encourage 56, 71
end-users 209
engage 97, 123
engagement 44, 62, 75, 121, 181
enhance 67
enhanced 100
enough 7, 79, 81, 91, 136, 150, 153, 206
ensure 30-31, 43, 61, 78, 82, 85, 90, 99-100, 116, 132, 141, 143, 146, 167, 177, 182, 220
ensures 85
ensuring 9, 95, 103, 147
entered 162
Enterprise 109
Entities 39
Entitled 196
entity 1
equipment 20, 146, 168
equipped 33
equitably 26
equivalent 212
errors 20, 77, 141, 171, 210
essential 64, 155
Essentials 96
establish 54, 174-175
estimate 35-36, 41, 145, 199, 216
estimated 24, 29, 35, 96, 120, 166, 173, 184
estimates 3-4, 27, 37, 51, 104-105, 125, 155, 170, 185-186, 199, 212
Estimating 4, 6, 123, 173-174, 216
estimation 59, 103-104, 106
ethical 26, 79, 145-146, 179
ethnic 78
European 132
evaluate 58, 62, 190
evaluated 188
evaluating 59

evaluation   60, 68, 108, 126, 196-198
evaluators   196
events 38, 57, 169, 190, 220
everyday   52
everyone   26, 30
everything   215
evidence   11, 41, 109, 122
evolution   34
evolve 71
exactly 146, 148
Example   2, 8, 13, 20, 48, 75
examples   7-8, 10
exceed   113, 130
exceeding   143
excellence   7, 91, 94
excellent   42
excelling   143
except 171
exclude   59
Exclusions   105
execute   136, 153
executed   34, 36, 194
executing   3, 105, 135, 139
execution   111, 134-135
executive   7, 82
executives   80
Exercise   130
existence   128
existing 10, 38, 45, 75, 81, 162, 198, 208, 220
expect 187, 216
expected   20, 30, 78, 90, 132, 147, 210, 215, 226
expecting   205
expend   38
expenses   183
expensive   40
experience   77, 84, 152, 184, 208
experiment   86
Expert 8
expertise   199
experts 25
explain 112, 122
explained   10
explicit 177

explicitly   90
explore   48
expressed   198
extent 11, 26, 61, 103-104
external   31, 98-99, 146, 168, 171
facilitate   11, 20, 72, 196
facing 17, 80
factors 38, 40, 54, 63, 78, 84, 98, 103, 117, 174, 220
failed   36
failing   93
failure   41, 91, 129, 142
fairly   26
falling   166
familiar 8
fashion 1, 31
Favorable   171, 208
feasible   40, 48, 93, 174, 193
feature 9
features   175
feedback   2, 10, 29, 32, 36
figure   44
finalize 155
finalized   13
finally   149
financial   43, 50-51, 97, 104, 121, 135, 151
fingertips   9
finish   117-118, 150, 164, 166, 216, 219
fiscal   94, 115
flowery 150
flying   27
focused   111
focuses   210
follow   10, 74, 94-95, 130
followed   28, 105, 141, 185, 212
following   8, 11, 177
follow-on   153
for--and   66
forecasts   166
foreseen   132
forever 100
forget 9
formal 4, 99, 123, 145, 193, 213, 222
formally   26, 29, 121, 141, 151, 186, 190

242

format 10, 192
formed 25, 31, 224
forming 142
formula 12, 87
Formulate 23
formulated 182, 185
forward 94, 96
foster 84, 95, 122
fosters 26
framework 72, 98, 178
freaky 81
frequency 30, 71, 108, 129
frequent 161
frequently 37, 43
friend 80, 88
fulfill 89
full-blown 41
full-scale 62
function 138, 156, 161, 192
functions 30, 47, 93, 99, 125, 134, 143, 158, 169, 185, 203
funded 153-154, 188
funding 91, 99, 154, 170
further 121
future 7, 41, 43, 73, 103, 112, 121, 147, 198
gained 50, 70, 72
gather 11, 34, 85
Gathering 157
General 111, 145
generally 110
generate 46, 50, 57
generated 46, 56
generation 8
geographic 138, 183
Gerardus 8
getting 28, 142
glamor 27
global 64, 87, 118
govern 89
governance 81, 103, 112, 115, 143
governing 139
granted 187
graphs 8, 39
gratitude 8

greater 103
grievances 62
ground 41, 50
groups 92, 105, 109, 142, 180, 186, 203
growth 53, 78
guaranteed 26
guidance 1, 147
Guidelines 198
handle 129, 134, 159, 175
handled 179
happen 19, 121, 128, 146
happening 87, 128
happens 7, 10, 83, 91, 99, 108, 116, 128, 163, 174
hardest 35
hardly 189
hardware 126, 151
hazards 128-129
HCISSP 1-6, 8-14, 16-22, 24-31, 33-43, 45, 47, 49-55, 57-61, 63-64, 66-72, 74-77, 79-107, 109-117, 119-121, 123-128, 130, 132-139, 141-143, 145-146, 149-155, 157, 159, 161-164, 166-171, 173, 175-177, 179-182, 184-192, 194-196, 198, 200-203, 205-206, 208-214, 216-218, 220-226
health 63
healthy 129
hearing 78
helpdesk 193
helpful 40, 191
helping 7
higher 107
high-level 24, 28, 112, 157, 220
highlight 122, 144
highly 98
high-tech 89
hijacking 77
hinder 141
hiring 59, 72
historical 132, 173, 208
history 125, 218
hitters 48
hitting 189
honest 79
humans 7
hypotheses 46

identified	1, 19, 27, 32-33, 38-40, 42-43, 49, 51, 105, 122-123, 128, 143, 157, 161, 179, 185, 190-191, 213
Identifier	220
identify	11, 16, 18, 21, 37-38, 44, 48-49, 51, 125, 139, 170-171, 174, 220
ignoring	80
images	158
imbedded	70
immediate	41
impact	4, 30, 32, 36-38, 41-42, 44, 58, 79, 103, 121, 155, 168-169, 175, 190, 194-195, 210, 225
impacted	111, 142, 162
impacting	201
impacts	141-142, 152, 180
implement	21, 38, 66
implicit	76
important	21, 40, 50, 53, 59, 81, 88, 100, 103-104, 107, 116, 126, 187
improve	2, 10-11, 39, 49, 54-64, 107, 134, 136
improved	54, 56, 59-61, 72, 103, 205
improving	55, 110
incentive	75
incentives	72
incident	215
include	59, 164, 186
included	2, 8, 158, 162, 173, 197, 216
includes	9, 42
including	18, 24-25, 30, 43, 49, 64, 67, 74, 141, 196, 220
in-coming	179
increase	61, 79
increased	144
increasing	82, 214
incurring	171
in-depth	11
indicate	43, 69, 77, 96
indicated	69
indicators	19, 35, 37, 45, 50, 53, 62, 74, 151, 170
indirect	155, 170-171
indirectly	1
individual	1, 40, 104, 124, 183, 185, 196, 216
industry	79, 83-84, 111, 146
infected	129
infection	129

infinite 87
influence   98, 144, 181, 214
influences   118, 140
informal   222
informed   83
ingrained   71
inhibit 56
initial   80
initiated   107, 162, 173, 195
Initiating   5, 99, 141, 210
Initiation   119
initiative   11, 139, 177, 220
Innovate   54
innovation   49, 52, 64, 68, 74, 95
innovative   98, 104, 136, 173, 216
inputs 24, 31, 47, 73, 125
insight 46, 51
insights 8
inspired   91
Instead86
insure 96
integrate   77
Integrated   151, 188
integrity   82, 194
intended   1, 57, 60
INTENT 16, 23, 34, 46, 54, 66, 76, 146
intention   1
intentions   146
interact   93
interest109, 140
interested   138
interests   37-38, 139
interface   151
interfaces   141
interim 97, 172
internal   1, 31, 84, 96, 99, 105, 141, 170
interpret   11-12
intervals   105
interview   83
introduced   27, 162
intuition   36
invaluable   2, 8, 10
inventory   156

investment 18, 94, 175, 178
invoices 111
involve 88
involved 17, 47, 55, 98, 109, 123, 137-139, 142, 158, 162, 167-168, 171, 180, 191
involves 70
isolate 34, 171
issues 57, 121, 123, 130, 134, 159, 162, 183, 201, 221
issuing 197
iteration 185
iterative 157
itself 1, 20
joining 162
journey 85
judgment 1
justified 142
kicked 86
killer 98
knock-on 121
knowledge 10, 31, 35, 42, 50, 67-68, 70, 72, 75, 84, 86, 93, 143, 163, 188
labeled 191
lacked 84
largely 52
latest 8
leader 20, 28, 49, 52, 183
leaders 26, 30-31, 39, 49, 81-83, 92, 140, 179
leadership 25, 32, 64, 93, 161, 182
learned 3, 74, 76, 119, 145, 177, 187, 205
learning 67-68, 214
legally 146
length 129
lessons 3, 62, 74, 76, 119, 145, 177, 187
letter 197
levels 18, 29, 50, 53, 73, 84, 113, 128, 168, 190
leverage 31, 64, 74, 77, 173
leveraged 31
levers 223
liability 1
licensed 1
lifecycle 36
Lifetime 9
likelihood 57-58, 103, 128

likely 74, 88, 169, 187, 214
limited 10, 144
linear 157
linked 28
listed 1, 178, 200
listen 91, 98
locally 167
located 167
location 138, 215
locations 179
logged 192
logical 159, 208
longer 72
long-range 92
long-term 70, 79, 92
losses 41
lowest 130
machines 126
magnitude 57
maintain 66, 78, 82, 188
maintained 146, 166, 202
makers 67, 210
making 20, 52, 59, 62, 81-82
Manage 38, 49, 93, 97, 111, 118, 127, 133, 137, 139, 151, 155, 168, 171, 177, 198, 206, 210, 225
manageable 28
managed 7, 24, 116, 132, 145, 161, 192
Management 1-6, 10-11, 18, 21, 24-25, 31, 35, 42, 55, 61, 64, 75, 77, 93, 96, 104-105, 109, 111-112, 115-116, 121, 123-124, 126, 134, 139-141, 145-146, 149, 151, 153, 155, 161-163, 166-167, 169, 171, 175, 179, 185-187, 189, 197-198, 200-201, 205, 208, 212, 214, 218, 222, 226
manager 7, 10, 21, 24, 31, 86, 109, 119, 123, 145, 149, 155, 186
managers 2, 102, 151, 166, 171, 191
Manages 198
Managing 2, 8, 102, 181
mandatory 195
manner 135, 145, 155, 170
manpower 112
mantle 81
mapped 26
marked 161

market 37, 74, 117, 121, 127, 189, 208, 220
marketable   121
marketer   7
Marketing   91, 100, 117
master 200
material   107, 171, 179, 191
materials   1, 105, 119, 182
matrices   206
Matrix 3-5, 137, 175, 190, 206
matter 25, 35, 45, 127
matters   214
mature 150
maximizing   88
meaning   116, 218
meaningful   42, 98
measurable   29, 83, 112
measure   2, 11, 17-18, 25, 31, 34-37, 39-43, 47, 49, 54, 58-59, 63, 68, 71-73, 108, 173-174, 208, 220
measured   21, 34-35, 38-42, 44, 64, 66, 73, 128, 190
measures   37-40, 43-45, 49-51, 53, 63, 69, 73, 104, 121, 136, 177
mechanical   1
mechanisms   177
mediated   183
medium   127, 189
meeting   26, 37, 74, 109, 133, 177, 182, 214
meetings   26, 28, 32, 105, 119, 151, 191, 210
megatrends   79
member   3, 6, 32, 89, 109, 139, 183, 197, 224
members   25-26, 28, 30, 106, 119, 125, 134, 139, 161, 167-168, 182-183, 191
memorable   107
message   222
method   27, 92, 104, 127, 140, 155, 175, 192, 218, 222
methods   30, 32, 40, 44, 173, 223
metrics 2, 29, 44, 72, 107-108, 186
milestone   3, 105, 117, 124, 131, 212, 220
milestones   24, 105, 166, 181, 219
Minimize   103, 151
minimizing   88
minimum   23, 184
minutes   26, 56, 133
missed 37, 78

Missing 89, 218
mission 48, 50, 78, 80-81, 83, 92, 146
mitigate 121, 161
mitigation 111, 168, 185
modeling 52, 178, 210
models 51, 82, 100
modern 106
modified 60, 170, 192
module 201
moments 51
momentum 78, 80
monetary 18, 226
monitor 60, 68-69, 71-72, 174
monitored 74, 217
Monitoring 6, 67, 73, 151, 159, 226
months 56, 58, 188
motivation 68, 73, 137
motive 177
moving 96
multiple 147, 209
myself 77
narrow 53
national 128
nearest 12
nearly 100
necessary 45, 47, 51, 56, 67, 82, 98, 147, 174, 191, 194
needed 19-21, 31, 47, 60, 68, 70, 72, 111, 136, 155, 173, 178, 210, 212, 221-222, 225
negatively 111
negotiate 86
negotiated 92, 222
neither 1
network 3, 130, 200, 222
Neutral 11, 16, 23, 34, 46, 54, 66, 76
normal 71, 129, 171
Notice 1
noticing 215
notified 139, 192
notify 182
number 22, 33, 39, 45, 53, 64, 75, 101, 175, 190, 203, 218, 227
numbers 182
objective 7, 44, 176, 188, 212, 220

objectives   16-17, 21, 23, 28, 30, 39, 48, 50, 70, 91, 96-97, 100, 109, 111, 115-116, 121, 128, 133, 142, 146, 188, 198, 210
observed   62
obsolete   79
obstacles   17, 138, 173, 216
obtain 98, 145
obtained   29, 44
obvious   81
obviously   12
occurring   63, 169, 175-176
occurs 22, 70, 103, 169
offerings   53, 59
offeror 196
offerors 196
Office   105, 109, 179, 187
officers 197
onboarding   111
one-time   7
ongoing   43, 55, 73, 217
online   10
on-site 133
opened   191
operate   128, 183, 188
operates   79
operating   5, 70, 182, 192
operation   70, 216
operations   10, 71-72, 188
operators   74, 107
opponent   214
opponents   139
opposite   79, 90
opposition   82
optimal   61-62, 184, 197
optimize   116
optimized   94
option 81
options 21, 125
orders   123
organism   129
organize   198
orient   74
oriented   167
orienting   119

origin   157
original 19, 147, 166, 170
originally   141
originate   67
others   105, 107, 121, 140, 143, 147, 173-174, 187-188, 200, 210, 214
otherwise   1, 56, 187
outcome   12, 120, 203
outcomes   36, 44, 58, 61, 88, 173, 205, 216
outlined   70
output 31, 42, 69
outputs   24, 47, 73, 147, 160
outside 56, 91, 136, 210, 220
Outsource   135, 163
overall 11-12, 17, 83, 104, 116, 120, 130, 154, 184, 210, 223
overcome   173, 216
overhead   171-172, 190-191
overheads   105
overlooked   210
overseas   168
oversight   105, 141
overtime   159
owners 113
ownership   27, 75
package   190
packages   190
paragraph   89
parallel   131
parameters   75, 179
Pareto 48
parking   111
particular   40, 48
partners   17, 43, 79, 92-93, 104, 135, 168
pattern   169
paycheck   83
paying 79
payment   105, 112, 137
peanut 145
pending   195
people 7, 19, 42, 50, 55, 58, 71, 74, 76-77, 86-87, 91, 93, 95, 98-100, 107, 109, 112, 125, 136, 139, 151, 153, 175-176, 189, 191, 209
perceived   175
percent   85, 96

percentage 206
perception 54, 60, 79
perform 19, 26-27, 30, 165, 203
performed 55, 105, 133, 164, 206, 208
performing 116, 136, 197, 210
perhaps 189
period 59
periods 193
permission 1
person 1, 117, 139
personally 206
personnel 18, 74, 177, 186, 200
pertinent 74
phases 36, 104, 154, 219
picked 92
placed 190
places 196
planet 71, 74
planned 34, 36, 68-70, 121, 136, 159, 190, 205
planners 67
planning 2, 8, 103, 109, 119, 130, 149, 159-160, 162, 180, 185, 204, 210
Planning- 70
Pocket 173
Pockets 174
points 22, 33, 45, 53, 64, 75, 101
policies 84, 138, 198, 222
policy 30, 67, 112, 159, 220
Political 56, 94
portfolio 3, 81, 115-116
portfolios 115, 139
portion 200
portray 48
position 143, 185
positioned 174
positions 138
positive 58, 78, 139, 223
positively 111
possible 36, 42, 50, 53, 56-57, 66, 81, 87, 126, 147
potential 17, 23, 38, 44, 59, 62-63, 77, 79, 87, 121, 128, 139, 162, 170, 197, 226
practical 48, 54, 57, 66, 109-110
practice 44

practices	1, 10, 72, 74-75, 106, 119
precaution	1
Predictive	203
predictor	190, 203
predictors	193
prefer	128
preferred	222
pre-filled	8
prepare	125, 144
preparing	200
present	43, 73, 149, 179
presented	192
presenting	147
preserve	32
pressures	118
prevent	20, 41, 121, 142, 171, 212
prevents	20
previous	31, 107, 153, 184, 200-201
previously	122, 152, 194, 198
pricing	196
primarily	111
primary	203
principles	82, 106, 198
printing	8
priorities	37, 39, 43, 187, 224
privacy	29, 74, 198
problem	16, 18-19, 21, 23-24, 26, 29, 31, 48, 50, 109, 192
problems	16-17, 19, 21, 34, 56, 59, 63, 69, 78, 157, 178
procedure	183
procedures	10, 68, 70, 74, 159, 170-171, 177, 185, 200, 222
proceeding	216
process	1-7, 10, 24, 27-28, 30-31, 34, 36, 38-39, 42-53, 60-62, 67, 69, 71-75, 103-104, 111, 115, 125-126, 133-135, 142, 149-150, 153, 157, 159, 161-162, 166, 168, 177-178, 201, 205-206, 210, 214, 220, 226
processes	26, 41, 47, 49-52, 68, 72, 75, 123, 141-142, 146, 153, 178, 194, 210, 212
produce	109, 133, 160, 210
produced	58, 119, 135
produces	218
producing	146, 206
product	1, 10, 35, 50, 53, 89-90, 98, 107, 109-110, 117, 119, 121, 129, 133-134, 145, 149-150, 154, 162, 188, 194, 209

production   55, 141
products   1, 17, 20, 42, 85, 103, 109, 151, 168, 194, 206, 220
profile 121
program   22, 59, 104, 116, 121, 143, 151, 185, 220
programme   103, 135-136
programs   109, 139, 192
progress   31, 34, 58, 78, 81-82, 103, 111, 119, 174, 211, 220
prohibited   171
Project 2-8, 19, 21, 26, 41, 47, 67, 70, 84, 86, 88, 91, 94, 96, 98-99, 102-107, 109-117, 119-121, 123-126, 130, 132, 134-138, 141-143, 145, 149-155, 161-162, 164, 166-169, 173, 175, 180-181, 184-190, 192, 194-195, 198, 200-203, 205-206, 209-213, 216-218, 220-221, 223, 226
Projected   170-171, 188, 191
Projection   176
Projects   2, 77, 85, 102-104, 109-110, 113, 119, 132, 139, 161, 166, 169, 175, 182, 189, 206, 209, 220
promising   98
promote   26, 42, 50, 125
promotion   144
proofing   62
Proper 116
properly   10, 24, 30, 45, 147, 157, 190, 211
proponents   139
Proposal   119
proposals   67, 126, 197
proposed   21, 36, 61, 121, 149, 153, 184, 196-198
protect   48, 79, 198
protection   88
protests   197
protocols   124
provide   22, 51, 87, 90, 99, 103, 105, 125, 135, 149, 155, 170, 173, 181, 191, 216
provided   8, 12, 69, 105, 119, 167
provides   117, 204
providing   119, 147, 181
provision   185
published   105, 196, 222
publisher   1
pulled 85
purchase   8, 10, 123, 133, 196
purchased   10, 124

purpose	2, 10, 92, 112, 174, 177, 182, 190, 193, 201, 203, 214, 220
purposes	105, 198
pursued	77
pushing	81
qualified	26, 213
qualifying	200
quality	1-2, 4, 10, 36, 40, 44, 47, 50, 68, 73, 105-108, 112, 134-135, 143-144, 146, 162, 177, 179-180, 192, 200, 212
question	11-12, 16, 23, 34, 46, 54, 66, 76, 83, 145, 178
questions	7-8, 11, 48, 216
quickly	10, 48-49, 52
radically	52
ranking	193
rather	83
rational	170
rationale	212, 215
reaching	91
reaction	176
reactivate	86
Readiness	222
readings	69, 103
re-align	115-116
realised	132
realism	196
realistic	127, 175
reality	146, 187
realized	85
really	7, 101
reason	90-91, 122, 222
reasonable	96, 105, 124, 166, 198, 212
reasons	25, 107
reassess	185
re-assign	219
rebuild	98
recasts	155
receipt	171
receive	8-9, 24, 39, 137, 223
received	31, 94
recent	168
recently	10, 82
recipient	163
recognize	2, 16, 18, 22, 61

recognized   17, 21, 59
recognizes   21
recommend   80, 88, 162
record 177
recorded   213
recording   1, 182
records   18, 47, 123-124, 170, 179
recovery   142
recruiting   147
Recurrence   128
redefine   27, 32
re-design   47
reduce 214
reduced   128
reducing   75, 82
references   227
reflect 50, 166
reform 37, 67, 93
reforms 21, 36, 41
regard 104
regarding   80, 110, 142, 196
Register   3-4, 121-122, 181, 225
regret 62
regular 28, 31, 161
regularly   26, 30, 32, 115, 210
regulated   192
regulatory   134, 179
reimbursed   183
reinforce   75
reject 149, 222
rejecting   149
relatable   170
relate 194
related 42, 44, 67, 139, 143, 189
relation   19, 92, 137
relations   99, 122
relative 186
relatively   99
release 107, 141, 150, 185
relevant   10, 29, 39, 51, 72, 79, 132, 134, 144, 175, 187
reliable 33
remain 146
remaining   174, 200, 205

remedial 41
remedies 41
remove 57
remunerate 61
repeatable 168
rephrased 10
replace 153
replanning 170
Report 3, 5, 45, 69, 109, 117, 134, 184, 202
reported 161
reporting 68, 108, 125, 170-171, 185
Reports 39, 119, 181, 192, 198
represent 64, 153, 194
reproduced 1
reputation 97
request 5, 48, 149, 187, 192-195
requested 1, 59, 192, 195
Requests 192
require 41, 75, 121, 152, 159, 220
required 20, 24, 26, 29, 33, 58, 63, 103, 118, 123, 126, 130, 149, 158, 182, 201, 218
requires 26
requiring 181
research 98, 147, 168
reserved 1
reserves 166
Resolution 51, 183
resolve 182, 219
resolved 183, 201
resource 3-5, 8, 99, 103, 109, 111, 115-116, 124, 152, 159, 166, 185-186, 203-204, 212, 218-219
resourced 147
resources 2, 8, 18, 25, 33, 37, 58, 64, 67, 72, 84, 87, 90, 95, 106, 118, 127, 130, 136-138, 147, 167, 173, 198, 200, 203, 218-219
Resourcing 116
respect 1
respond 122
responded 12
response 22, 67-70
responsive 173
result 51, 58, 64, 108, 111, 162, 173, 195, 222
resulted 72
resulting 50, 103, 111, 162, 170

results 8, 30, 41, 53-54, 57-59, 61, 69, 73, 103, 105, 125, 145-146, 148, 156, 173, 196, 200, 210
Retain 76
retained   112
retention   62
retrospect   85
return 43, 58, 131, 178
returned   27
revenue   36, 44
review 10, 115, 119, 146, 191, 193, 199-200, 215
reviewed   30, 121, 141, 161-162
reviews 10, 105, 124, 224
revise 115
revised 51, 72, 128
revisit 215
reward 40, 42, 51, 75, 109
rewards   72
rework 20
rights 1
risk-based   116
roadmaps   28
robustness   117
routine 68
safeguard   138
safely 129
safety 62-63, 85, 183
sample 179
samples   179
Sampling   179
satisfied   89, 94, 98, 119, 145
satisfy 210
satisfying   97
savings 27, 51
scaled 166
schedule   4-5, 29, 64, 74, 91, 105-106, 111, 133-134, 152, 166, 170-171, 190, 194, 197, 199-201, 205
scheduled   106, 150, 210
Schedules   126, 190, 200
scheduling   167
scheme   67
Scorecard   2, 12-14
scorecards   72
Scores 14

scoring 10
seamless 96
second 12
section 12, 22, 33, 45, 53, 64, 75, 101
sector 189
Secure 95
Securing 96
security 17, 29, 63, 71, 74, 107, 141, 181, 194
seemed 126
segment 222
segmented 33
segments 33, 92
select 48
selected 57, 61, 168, 173-174, 185, 198, 224
selecting 93, 183
Selection 5, 196
seller 196
sellers 1
selling 81, 214
senior 26, 39, 92, 179
separated 190
sequence 164
sequencing 93, 103
series 11
servers 126
service 1-2, 7-8, 10, 35, 54, 60, 84, 98, 109-110, 117, 119, 121, 162, 188
services 1, 8, 42-43, 90, 155-156, 163, 184
session 149
setbacks 49, 52
several 8, 115
severely 47
shared 72, 104, 157, 173, 182
sharing 67, 223
shortest 126
should 7, 18, 27-28, 38-39, 48, 51, 55, 60-61, 64, 67, 71, 73, 86, 91, 95, 98-100, 103, 117, 121-122, 125, 137, 143-144, 151, 162, 164, 168, 181, 192-193, 195-197, 201, 203, 208, 211, 217, 219, 224
-should 187
showing 185
signature 82
signatures 159
similar 26, 31, 48, 53, 59, 107, 125, 132, 218

simple 99, 189
simply 8, 10, 214
single 89, 171, 183
single-use 7
situation 20, 34, 121, 136, 189, 212
skeptical 100
skills 18, 37, 45, 84, 86, 88, 111, 135, 151, 226
slippage 168
smallest 18, 58
social 91, 100, 128
societal 89, 99
software 20, 106, 125-126, 150-151, 169, 186
solicit 32
soluiton 184
solution 44, 48, 51, 54-59, 61-62, 64, 66
solutions 38, 41, 45, 56-57, 59-60, 62
Someone 7
something 100, 175
Sometimes 41
Source 5, 99, 141, 196
sources 48, 57, 85
special 8, 69, 221-222
specific 8, 18, 20, 29-30, 94, 109, 111, 117, 143, 159, 185, 194, 212, 218
specified 91, 129, 132, 154, 170-171
spoken 82
Sponsor 21, 133, 161, 212, 222
sponsored 28
sponsors 17, 134, 210
stability 45, 108
stable 150, 152, 209
staffed 25
staffing 18, 72, 185, 213
stages 186
stakes 137
standard 7, 159, 208
standards 1, 10-11, 71, 86, 107, 132, 141-142, 177, 194
started 8, 130
starting 11, 115
startup 79, 221
stated 90, 93, 157
statement 4, 11, 56, 59, 87, 155, 161-162, 185

statements   12, 22, 24, 29, 33, 45, 50, 53, 64, 75, 101, 146-147, 150, 178
status   3, 5, 50, 105, 109, 111, 115, 134, 137, 161, 166, 184, 189, 211, 225
statutory   134
Steering   141
storage   177, 192
strategic   99-100, 115-116, 121, 147, 220
strategies   82, 111, 214
strategy   17, 60, 74, 77, 83, 87, 90, 112, 197, 208
strengths   117, 183
strong 144
stronger   96
Strongly   11, 16, 23, 34, 46, 54, 66, 76
Structure   3, 5, 33, 64, 81, 98, 113, 185, 197, 203
stubborn   86
stupid 95
subject 8-9, 25
subjective   150
Submit 10, 192
submitted   10, 194
subsequent   115
subset 18
subtotals   155
succeed   79, 117
success   18, 21, 25, 35, 39-42, 58, 66, 77-78, 84, 87, 91, 96, 98, 104, 110, 124, 153-154, 167, 215, 220
successful   53, 61, 70, 84, 86-87, 91, 110, 135, 140, 187, 220, 222
sufficient   41, 112, 135
suggest   151, 193
suggested   69, 194
suitable   39, 133, 169, 171
supervisor   144, 183
supplier   93, 168
suppliers   24, 43, 48, 93
Supply 117, 168
support   7, 52, 56, 70, 74-75, 82, 90, 147, 151, 159, 183, 190, 196, 220
supported   25, 50
supporting   63, 177
supportive   106, 144
supports   183

surface 69
Surveys 8
SUSTAIN 2, 76
sustaining 70, 182
symptom 16
system 10-11, 48, 67-68, 75, 77, 93, 141, 147, 150, 157-158, 170, 191, 194, 209
systematic 43
systems 42, 49, 51, 72, 84, 93, 135, 148, 189, 208, 223
tackled 93
tactics 214
tailor 222
taking 36, 44, 109
talents 84, 111
talking 7
target 25, 107, 212, 222
targets 63, 112, 189, 220
tasked 75
technical 56, 141, 176, 193, 199
techniques 51, 82, 185, 210
technology 84, 98, 117, 152, 157, 168, 182
template 200-201
templates 7
testable 158
Test-Cycle 178
tested 17, 56, 179, 223
testing 59, 61, 107, 141
thankful 8
thematic 138
themselves 87, 96
theory 68, 73
therein 191
things 57, 136, 162, 226
thinking 49, 56
thorough 195
thought 140
threat 90
Threats 128, 142
through 28, 47, 93, 162, 215
throughout 1, 83
tighter 100
time-bound 29
timeframe 174, 218

timeline 194, 226
timely 31, 119, 134-135, 155, 170, 175
Timescales 118
timetable 130
timing 175
together 98
tolerable 128
tomorrow 71, 74, 83
top-down 72
totally 94
touched 157
toward 74, 109
towards 51
tracked 105, 162
tracking 24, 185, 211
traction 100
trademark 1
trademarks 1
tradeoff 197
trained 25, 28, 30, 168
training 19, 21, 58, 68-69, 72, 110, 135, 141, 143, 147, 188, 198, 222, 224
Transfer 12, 22, 33, 45, 53, 64, 72, 75, 101, 188
transition 149, 151
translated 29
trends 18, 50, 53, 128, 168-169
Tricky 88
trophy 81
trouble 79
trying 7, 51, 77, 94, 128, 222
turnaround 218
ubiquitous 87
ultimate 94
underlying 63
undermine 94
understand 32, 143, 150, 200
understood 84, 94, 157
undertake 52, 121
underway 60, 220
uninformed 83
unique 182
unknown 128
Unless 7

unlike   152
unproven   151
unresolved   159
updated   8-9, 50, 130, 161, 212
updates   9, 72, 125
upfront 223
upload 182
usability   77
useful   63, 73, 114, 121
usefully 11, 18
UserID   117
utilized 119, 170
utilizing 58
validated   24, 28, 30, 46, 119
valuable   7
values   83, 92-93, 128, 179
variables   42, 51, 69, 214
variance   5, 127, 191, 208
-variance   187
variances   171, 185, 208
variation   16, 30, 34, 36, 38-39, 48, 75
variety 58
various 186
Vendor 111, 124, 151
vendors   17, 100
verified 9, 24, 28, 30, 46
verify   71, 73, 162, 188
Version 227
versions   27, 31
versus   183
Veterans   216
viable   113
Violation   141
Virgin   27
vis-à-vis   168
vision   83, 87, 92-93
visions   104
visualize   216
voices   181
volatile 64
volatility   152
volume   208
volunteers   183

warrant 133
warranty 1, 192
wealth 37, 45
website 193
whether 7, 70, 80, 146, 220
willing 175, 187
window 218
within 52, 59, 110, 128, 145, 183, 185, 190, 194, 217-218
without 1, 12, 40, 78, 98, 116, 166, 194, 201
worked 55, 111, 179
workers 78
workflow 214
workforce 18, 44, 62-63, 75, 92-93, 97
working 60, 69-70, 143, 209, 215
workplace 63
Worksheet 4, 6, 173, 216
writing 10, 207
written 1
yourself 47, 89, 135, 144

CPSIA information can be obtained
at www.ICGtesting.com
Printed in the USA
FSHW011104250119
55256FS